HOW TO
RECEIVE

YOUR
MIRACLE

FROM
GOD

HOW TO RECEIVE
YOUR
MIRACLE
FROM GOD

DAVID CERULLO

Copyright © 2007

David Cerullo

Inspiration Ministries
P.O. Box 7750
Charlotte, NC 28241 USA

www.inspiration.org

ISBN Number: 978-1-887600-89-7

All Scripture passages are from the New American Standard Bible,
unless otherwise noted.

New American Standard Bible © The Lockman Foundation, 1960.

Printed in the United States of America.

DEDICATION

This book is dedicated to…

…Ministers of the Gospel around the world who believe Jesus Christ is the same yesterday, today, and forever.

…Those who believe we serve a Miracle-Working God Who continues to demonstrate His love and power by stepping into the circumstances of our lives in miraculous ways today.

…Those who desperately need a miracle.

May this book cause you to experience a Divine encounter with your Heavenly Father and help you receive the miracle you need from Him.

God bless you.

TABLE OF CONTENTS

YOUR APPOINTMENT WITH A MIRACLE

GOD IS A GOD OF MIRACLES!

He is the Lord God Almighty, and the entire universe was created by the power of His spoken word. His very character and nature is miraculous. He rules over the heavens and the earth, and *nothing* is too difficult for Him.

This same God is *your* Heavenly Father. He loves you, cares about you, and wants good things for you. As a child of God, you have access to *all* He is and possesses, including His miracle-working power.

God has never stopped stepping into the circumstances of people's lives with His mighty, life-changing miracles, and *you* can experience a miracle from Him today!

Do YOU Need a Miracle?

So many people are bombarded with overwhelming problems: overdue bills that need paying, crippling arthritis, a mother who has just been diagnosed with incurable cancer, an abusive spouse, rebellious children, unsaved grandchildren—the list of heartaches, tragedies, and painful circumstances seems endless.

When we look into the faces of our loved ones, friends, or

strangers, we just don't know the heavy burdens they may be carrying. On the outside, their smiles can be masking their pain, and when we ask how things are going, their polite, "Fine," can be an attempt to hide deep hurts on the inside.

Meanwhile in their hearts, they're crying out to God in desperation, "Where *are* You? Why won't You help me? Where is *my* miracle?"

The truth is that *you* may be someone who is crying out for God to intervene with a miracle in the midst of *your* desperate situation.

My friend, you're not holding this book by accident. God has an ordained purpose for you to be reading these words, even at this very moment.

Jesus Is Our Healer

Everywhere Jesus went, miracles happened. Hungry people were fed. Sick people were healed. Demonized people were set free. Dead people came back to life.

Being around Jesus was never boring. But while He made many people glad, He made others mad. He was a threat to the status quo, and even more than that, He was a threat to Satan's kingdom: *"The Son of God appeared for this purpose, to destroy the works of the devil"* (1 John 3:8).

Every time I read the Gospels, I am always amazed by Jesus' compassion for people and His longing to give them the miracles they needed. Who else could ask a question like this: *"What do you want Me to do for you?"* (Mark 10:36, 51) *Whatever* the need, He was able to meet it.

Do you realize that Jesus is asking *you* this very same question today? He's reaching out His mighty hand and asking you, *"What do you want Me to do for you?"* He is inviting you to share the deepest needs of your heart.

How will you answer Him?

What kind of Divine miracle do you need from Him today?

God Wants to Prosper You!

I know many Christians who need a miracle, but they're afraid to ask God for one. If most Believers were honest, they would admit there is at least one area in their life they wish could be radically different. But nothing they've done has been able to bring about the change they need.

Some may be leery of asking for a miracle because of unbelief. They don't believe...

* ...in God.
* ...that He still performs miracles today.
* ...they are worthy of receiving a miracle.

But God isn't a respecter of persons, and He wants to prosper *you* in every area of your life:

*"Beloved, I pray that in **ALL** respects you may prosper and be in good health, just as your soul prospers"* (3 John 2).

To prosper means "to flourish, to succeed, to have wealth." God wants to make you completely whole in your relationships, finances, body, and spirit.

How can you know if it's YOUR time for a miracle? Because God says so!

*"For He says, 'AT THE ACCEPTABLE TIME I LISTENED TO YOU, AND ON THE DAY OF SALVATION I HELPED YOU.' Behold, **now** is 'THE ACCEPTABLE TIME,' behold, **now** is 'THE DAY OF SALVATION'"* (2 Corinthians 6:2).

God wants to save, help, and heal you *"now"!*

God's Deep Love for You

One of the best examples I can offer to communicate God's

loving, Father heart for you is to draw a parallel between Him and a loving, caring parent.

Would you as a loving, caring parent want to see your children poor, naked, starving, sick, bruised, broken, depressed, or lonely? Of course not. Wouldn't you do everything in your power to change their situation if you could? Certainly you would.

Haven't there been times when you wished you could suffer on your child's behalf so that he (or she) wouldn't have to bear pain or endure a desperate situation?

Well, this is exactly how our loving, caring Heavenly Father feels about *you*. He derives *NO* pleasure in seeing His children suffer. Isaiah 53 conveys His deep love for us:

"Surely our griefs He Himself bore, and our sorrows He carried; yet we ourselves esteemed Him stricken, smitten of God, and afflicted. But He was pierced through for our transgressions, He was crushed for our iniquities; the chastening for our well-being fell upon Him, and by His scourging we are healed" (vs. 4).

It's Time to Receive Your Miracle NOW!

Timing is an essential key to God's plans and purposes.

Scripture teaches that God makes Divine appointments for specific times to meet with His children. For example, He made dates on His "calendar" to meet with us to celebrate Passover, Pentecost, and the Feast of Tabernacles.

In John 11, there is a powerful story that emphasizes the importance of God's miraculous timing.

Jesus' good friend, Lazarus, had been dead for three days. He could have gone to heal Lazarus when He first heard that His friend was sick, but He waited until Lazarus had died.

Or He could have raised Lazarus the same day he died; instead He chose to wait for *two more days*, telling his disciples,

"Lazarus is dead, and I am glad for your sakes that I was not there, so that you may believe; but let us go to him" (vs. 14-15).

Jesus arrived at the right time, on the right day, to resurrect Lazarus. Why did He delay Lazarus' resurrection? To build their faith *"so that you may believe."*

The right timing for your miracle is *GOD'S* timing. It won't come a day early or a day late; you will receive your miracle at exactly the right time.

God *wants* to meet with you. God has a plan and a purpose for *you.* This is your hour.

Do you need a miracle in your family...your marriage... your finances...your physical body...your spirit?

Have you tried everything? Have you looked everywhere?

You may feel like all hell and the devil's demons have broken loose in your life, and that it's impossible for things to change.

Well, I want you to know that the devil is *not* in control of your life. All stress, depression, loneliness, anxiety, sickness, lack, or need is rooted in the devil exercising his power and authority over you and your circumstances, but God is able to set you FREE!

You may be thinking, "Well, it would take a miracle to set me free from my problems!" And that's *exactly* what God wants to give you today: a MIRACLE!

There's an old Sunday school song I've always loved:

Got any rivers you think are uncrossable?
Got any mountains you can't tunnel through?
God specializes in things thought impossible,
and does the things that others cannot do.
— Oscar C. Eliason

God's miracles are for you and me *NOW.* He is the same yesterday, today, and forever (Hebrews 13:8), and He continues to work miracles in the lives of His children every day.

It's my earnest prayer that your heart will be completely

open to what only God can do for you through His miracle-working power.

My friend, get ready to receive *YOUR* miracle!

CHAPTER ONE
TAKE AUTHORITY!

WHEN GOD CREATED MANKIND, He intended for us to have authority over the earth, and He has communicated through His Word the concept of our rulership, authority, and government:

> *"Let Us make man in Our image, according to Our likeness; and let them rule..."* (Genesis 1:26).

> *"God blessed them; and God said to them, 'Be fruitful and multiply, and fill the earth, and subdue it; and rule over the fish of the sea and over the birds of the sky and over every living thing that moves on the earth'"* (Genesis 1:28).

> *"You make him to rule over the works of Your hands; You have put all things under his feet"* (Psalm 8:6).

> *"The heavens are the heavens of the LORD, but the earth He has given to the sons of men"* (Psalm 115:16).

God clearly is telling us, "I want you to govern, rule, subjugate, subdue, and take possession of the earth!" He has assigned the earth to us...to be in charge of it, to guard it, and to protect it.

From the beginning of creation, God's intention has been for His children to manage the affairs of the earth. This means

He wants *you* to rule your personal world with your God-given authority.

Jesus Paid the Price

When Adam and Eve sinned in the Garden of Eden, they submitted to Satan instead of God, and by doing so, they delegated their God-given authority to him. *God* didn't give Satan authority over the earth, and He didn't give Satan authority over us…*we* granted him that authority through our sin.

Satan succeeded in gaining what he had been after all along…a kingdom. Jesus described Satan as the *"ruler of this world"* (John 14:30). From the moment that Adam and Eve chose to sin, the authority over this world was transferred from man to Satan. But God had a plan.

He knew that one day He would send His Son Jesus Christ into the world. He would also pay the ultimate price for our redemption and shed His guiltless blood to atone for the sins of the world. Through His sinless life, death, and resurrection, Jesus would take back the authority over the world from Satan and return it to us as God's appointed, rightful owners.

Isaiah prophesied, *"He was wounded for our transgressions, He was bruised for our iniquities; the chastisement of our peace was upon Him; and with His stripes we are healed. 'All we like sheep have gone astray; we have turned every one to his own way'; and the LORD hath laid on Him the iniquity of us all."* (Isaiah 53:5-6 KJV).

Jesus Came to Set Us Free!

When Jesus was here on earth, Satan came to Him and said, *"I will give you all this domain and its glory; for it has been handed over to me, and I give it to whomever I wish. Therefore if You worship before me, it shall all be Yours"* (Luke 4:6-7).

Satan was offering Jesus dominion and authority over the earth. It's clear that this authority had been given to Satan, and it's also clear that he could give it to whomever he wished. Where did Satan get this authority? From man!

But Jesus responded, *"It is written, 'YOU SHALL WORSHIP THE LORD YOUR GOD AND SERVE HIM ONLY'"* (Luke 4:8). Jesus Christ came into the world to set us free from Satan's authority, and that's exactly what He did.

Another day, the Lord entered a synagogue and said to the people there, *"THE SPIRIT OF THE LORD IS UPON ME, BECAUSE HE ANOINTED ME TO PREACH THE GOSPEL TO THE POOR, HE HAS SENT ME TO PROCLAIM RELEASE TO THE CAPTIVES, AND RECOVERY OF SIGHT TO THE BLIND, TO SET FREE THOSE WHO ARE OPPRESSED, TO PROCLAIM THE FAVORABLE YEAR OF THE LORD"* (Luke 4:18-19).

As Jesus hung on the Cross and spoke the words, *"It is finished"* (John 19:30), the price for our guilt was paid. He had atoned for our sins.

God looked at Jesus' blood covering the Mercy Seat in Heaven and declared it sufficient. At that moment, Jesus became the *new* Head over the earth, and Satan no longer had authority.

When God raised Jesus from the dead and seated Him at His right hand in Heaven, God placed His Son, *"far above all rule and authority and power and dominion, and every name that is named, not only in this age but also in the one to come. And He put all things in subjection under His feet, and gave Him as head over all things to the church"* (Ephesians 1:19b-22).

For this reason, He is *"the head over all rule and authority"* (Colossians 2:10).

Jesus Conquered Sin and Death

Jesus not only took our place in death: He conquered death itself.

In his letter to the Corinthians, the apostle Paul wrote, "*O death, where is thy sting? O grave, where is thy victory? The sting of death is sin; and the strength of sin is the law. But thanks be to God, which giveth us the victory through our Lord Jesus Christ*" (1 Corinthians 15:55-57 KJV).

Then in his letter to the Colossian church, Paul writes that through His Son's death, God has delivered us from the authority of darkness and transferred us to His Kingdom of love (1:13).

When Jesus stepped into the abyss of Hell and took the keys to the kingdom from Satan, He took back the authority Adam and Eve had transferred to the devil in the Garden of Eden (Ephesians 4:8-10; Revelations 1:8).

After His resurrection from the dead, Jesus spoke to His disciples and said, "*As the Father has sent Me, I also send you*" (John 20:21). How did God send Jesus into the world? With all authority! And how does Jesus send us into the world? With all authority!

Now please pay close attention to this:

Nowhere does the Bible teach that Jesus stripped the devil of his *power*. If that were the case, the devil could no longer impact or control us.

What Jesus *did* do was to strip Satan of his *authority*. We need to see the devil for who and what he really is: a deceiver and a thief who comes to steal, kill, and destroy (John 10:10). He is a usurper of authority who has NO RIGHT to steal, kill, and destroy.

Let me ask you something...

Are you living in the reality of your freedom in Jesus Christ? Are you walking in the knowledge of the truth that you have been set free from sin and death?

Are you grounded in the truth that you are no longer a resident of the devil's kingdom of darkness but are now living in the Kingdom of the Son of God's Love?

The Greatest Miracle

The greatest miracle of all time is the miracle of salvation that is only available to us when we choose to believe in Jesus Christ as our Savior and make Him the Lord of our lives.

Unless and until we make that choice, the sad truth is that we are ineligible to receive God's blessings, and we cannot access His miracle-working power.

God is holy. He is righteous. He is almighty. And He also is our loving Heavenly Father, Who desperately wants all of His children to come to Him through the saving blood of His Son.

"The Lord is not slow about His promise, as some count slowness, but is patient toward you, not wishing for any to perish but for all to come to repentance" (2 Peter 3:9).

If you're not a child of God, if you have never invited Christ to be the Lord of your life, then you are not a part of His "family," and you're not entitled to the benefits of being a joint heir with His Son.

While this doesn't mean a non-Christian couldn't experience a miracle from God, it does mean that only His children who have been saved from hell and "born again" into His family have the right to *expect* a miracle.

The Pearl of Great Price

When God saves us through the blood Jesus spilled on the Cross, He saves us from the punishment we deserve for our sins. But because of His great love for us, He saves us from even *more...*

To be saved by God is to be made totally whole: physically,

mentally, emotionally, and spiritually. He wants to cover us with His grace, His blessing, and His forgiveness.

The Bible refers to Jesus as our *"pearl of great price,"* the most precious jewel we can discover in the entire universe:

"The kingdom of heaven is like unto a merchant man, seeking goodly pearls: Who, when he had found one pearl of great price, went and sold all that he had, and bought it" (Matthew 13:45-46 KJV).

In His amazing love and mercy, Jesus gave His life on that blood-soaked Cross to redeem us from suffering an ever-lasting punishment in hell, eternally separated from God. We can *only* be saved from this by God's grace and Jesus' blood.

Asking Jesus Christ to be your Savior and the Lord of your life is simple. You do it by FAITH. You choose to believe that He is God's Son and that He alone can save you from your sins.

"And without faith it is impossible to please Him, for he who comes to God must believe that He is and that He is a rewarder of those who seek Him" (Hebrews 11:6).

If you haven't yet asked Jesus to be the Savior and Lord of your life, I want to show you through Scripture why you need Him and how you can receive the greatest miracle of all time, *right now.*

1. BELIEVE THAT GOD SENT JESUS TO EARTH TO SAVE SINNERS.

"It is not those who are healthy who need a physician, but those who are sick...for I did not come to call the righteous, but sinners" (Matthew 9:12-13).

2. ACKNOWLEDGE YOUR SIN.

"For all have sinned, and fall short of the glory of God" (Romans 3:23).

"God, be merciful to me, the sinner!"
(Luke 18:13)

3. CONFESS AND REPENT OF YOUR SIN.

"If we confess our sins, He is faithful and righteous to forgive us our sins and to cleanse us from all unrighteousness" (1 John 1:9).

4. BELIEVE ON JESUS CHRIST.

"For God so loved the world, that He gave His only begotten Son, that whoever believes in Him shall not perish, but have eternal life" (John 3:16).

"If you confess with your mouth Jesus as Lord, and believe in your heart that God raised Him from the dead, you will be saved; for with the heart a person believes, resulting in righteousness, and with the mouth he confesses, resulting in salvation" (Romans 10:9-10).

5. RECEIVE ETERNAL LIFE.

"But as many as received Him, to them He gave the right to become children of God, even to those who believe in His name" (John 1:12).

6. TURN AWAY FROM YOUR OLD WAYS.

"Let the wicked forsake his way, and the unrighteous man his thoughts: and let him return to the LORD, and He will have compassion on him; and to our God, for He will abundantly pardon" (Isaiah 55:7).

Are You Ready?

If you are ready to receive the greatest miracle of all time—

the miracle of sins forgiven and the gift of eternal life—then you can take care of that right now. Just pray this prayer:

Heavenly Father,

Thank You for Your great love for me. Please forgive me for all my sins. I believe that Jesus Christ is Your Son, that He died on the Cross for me, and that He rose from the dead. Please wash me clean with His blood. I thank you God for forgiving me and making me Your child.

Jesus, please come into my life right now, live in my heart, and fill me with Your Holy Spirit. Be the Lord of my life. Set me free now from every bondage that the devil has held in my life.

Jesus, I pray this prayer in Your powerful Name. Amen.

If you just prayed this prayer, then I welcome you into the family of God. Right now, the angels in Heaven are rejoicing over you! (Luke 15:10)

In the following days, weeks, and months, you'll begin to see God do exciting things in your life, because you are now a new creation in Him!

"If anyone is in Christ, he is a new creature; the old things passed away; behold, new things have come" (2 Corinthians 5:17).

With Jesus Christ as your Lord, you'll want to do His will, even when what *He* wants conflicts with what *you* want. When you find yourself tempted to rebel against Him, simply pray the same thing that He prayed to the Heavenly Father, *"Not **My** will, but **Yours** be done"* (Luke 22:42).

Because Jesus Christ is now the center of your life, you have His peace to protect you when you feel afraid. Although Satan will try to steal God's peace away from you, it can be restored just by calling on Jesus' name in faith and declaring Scriptures like this one over yourself: *"Peace I leave with you; My peace I give to you; not as the world gives do I give to you. Do not let your heart be troubled, nor let it be fearful"* (John 14:27).

God's Holy Spirit is inside you now, and this reflects the wondrous miracle of being born again into God's family…a real experience that has changed your life *forever.* He will guide you, comfort you, help you to resist the temptation to sin, and give you wisdom when making a decision:

"The Spirit Himself testifies with our spirit that we are children of God" (Romans 8:16). While you may experience times when you don't sense His Presence, just stand by faith upon the eternal promises in God's inerrant Word.

And now, my friend, you are able to expect *and* receive all of God's mighty, miracle-working power!

As a child of God, let me show you who you *really* are!

We Are Sons and Daughters of GOD!

Because Jesus has conquered sin and death, we are able to…

* Bind the forces of hell with authority!
* Pray with authority!
* Speak with authority!
* Expect our Heavenly Father to back up this God-given authority with His power!

We need to see ourselves for who we really are: Sons and Daughters of the Most High God, who have been given authority over *all* of the devil's power.

When Jesus healed the sick and cast devils out of people, it was said of Him, *"…for with authority and power he commandeth the unclean spirits, and they come out"* (Luke 4:36 KJV).

The Greek word used in this text for authority is *exousia,* which means "having the right or capability to exercise power."

What power? The supernatural, miracle-working power of God! And this is the same authority Jesus has delegated to *us*.

When Peter and John came upon a lame man lying near the Temple, they experienced this power in an amazing way:

"'I do not possess silver and gold, but what I do have I give to you: In the name of Jesus Christ the Nazarene—walk!' And seizing him by the right hand, he raised him up; and immediately his feet and his ankles were strengthened. With a leap he stood upright and began to walk; and he entered the temple with them, walking and leaping and praising God" (Acts 3:6-8).

What did Peter and John have? AUTHORITY! Authority to exercise the supernatural, miracle-working power of Jesus.

You Have Authority Over the Devil!

Since we have the same God-given authority that Jesus had, why do so many of us as Believers live under Satan's power of sin, sickness, and spiritual death? Why do so many of us allow the devil to influence—and even control—our lives and circumstances?

The answer could lie in the mistaken belief that the devil is not real and that his power is not real.

* It could lie in the mistaken belief that Jesus stripped Satan of his power, and he is now powerless.
* It could lie in the fact that many Christians don't understand Jesus has given us authority over all the devil's authority.
* It could lie in the fact that it's one thing to know you *have* authority, and it's another thing to *use* the authority you've been given.

As you read this book, please know that one of the greatest keys you have for experiencing your miracle is exercising your God-given authority over the circumstances the devil has brought into your life.

As you lay hold of this truth, get ready to receive a genuine miracle from God!

CHAPTER TWO
GOD SAID IT!

CAN WE REALLY BELIEVE WHAT the Bible says about miracles? *Can we?*

Absolutely! The Bible is the Word of *God.*

* It's the foundation on which we stand.
* It's the written Word of God.
* It's God's "Owner's Manual" for His creation.
* It's one of the only "absolutes" we can count on.
* It's our Heavenly Father's "love letter" to His precious kids.
* It's our primary source for believing in His miracle-working power.

God's Word is full of miracles!

Now, you may be thinking to yourself, "But how can I even trust that what the Bible says is true?" That's a great question!

Sound, Biblical Doctrine

With any teaching you may hear from the pulpit on Sunday, watch on Christian programming, listen to on Christian radio, or read in a Christian book, it's always vitally important to test what is being taught to see if it's based on sound, Biblical doctrine.

What is doctrine?

The word "doctrine" comes from the Latin word *doctrina,* which means "a body of teachings; instructions." Doctrine is basically a set of beliefs or teachings that a group of people accept as their authority. For us as Believers, God's Word is our doctrine.

There are three primary ways we can test for sound, Biblical doctrine:

1. Are there two or more witnesses?

In the Old Testament, God provided simple guidelines for believing someone's testimony: It had to be corroborated from the mouths of two or more people (Deuteronomy 17:6; 19:15).

Jesus reinforced this Scriptural mandate when He said, *"By the mouth of two or three witnesses every fact may be confirmed"* (Matthew 18:16).

So then for Scriptural doctrine to be trustworthy, it can't be taken out of context, and it must be supported in at least two places. God's Word must bear witness to itself, and this witness must be confirmed by the testimony of other credible witnesses.

2. Does the doctrine clearly support Scripture?

Mark 7:13 specifically warns us against *"invalidating the word of God by your tradition which you have handed down; and you do many things such as that."*

Ask yourself, "Does what is being taught support Scripture or contradict it?" Sadly, what is often preached as traditional, Biblical doctrine is actually an attempt to invalidate God's Word. If any teaching you're hearing or reading contradicts the Bible, it is wrong, and you must reject it.

3. Does the doctrine bear good fruit?

Matthew 7:15-18 has another sober warning for us: *"Beware of the false prophets, who come to you in sheep's clothing, but inwardly are ravenous wolves. You will know them by their fruits. So every good tree bears good fruit, but the bad tree bears bad fruit. A good tree cannot produce bad fruit, nor can a bad tree produce good fruit."*

So how can we know if a doctrine is true or false? By

the fruit the teaching bears. Is it bringing the *"righteousness and peace and joy in the Holy Spirit"* of God's Kingdom (Romans 14:17)?

If you are able to answer "yes" to these three questions, then you can trust that the doctrine being taught is Biblical truth. But if what you are hearing, seeing, or reading does *not* line up with Scripture, beware!

So how can we know if modern-day miracles are sound, Biblical doctrine?

* There are hundreds and thousands of witnesses living today who can joyfully testify to God's miracle-working power!
* Scripture is *FULL* of miracles, so the current-day miracles of God's healing power, His protection, and His supernatural provision testify that His Word is TRUTH!
* The amazing fruit of the Holy Spirit's righteousness, peace, and joy is being poured out on the multitudes of those who are receiving God's miraculous intervention in their lives!

In a later chapter, I'm going to share with you some powerful, faith-building testimonies of people who have experienced firsthand our loving Heavenly Father's wonder-working power. For right now, let me state this urgent truth to you as clearly as I can:

**If you desperately need a miracle,
you *MUST* be willing and determined to believe
what the Bible—the written, holy, inerrant Word of
Almighty God—says about miracles.**

Decide today that you will not *"live on bread alone, but on **every word** that proceeds out of the mouth of God"* (Matthew 4:4).

I Believe It!

Among strong, committed, overcoming Christians today,

there is a modern-day, widely-repeated proverb containing deep wisdom:

GOD SAID IT. I BELIEVE IT. THAT SETTLES IT!

If what someone teaches you in print or on television, radio, the internet, or in person on *any* subject is truly sound, Biblical doctrine, it will line up with the written Word of God.

If it doesn't, don't believe it!

If it does, believe it!

Our great God says, *"Heaven and earth will pass away, but My words shall not pass away"* (Matthew 24:35).

All He is asking us to do with the *"exceeding great and precious promises"* (2 Peter 1:4) He has made to us in His Word is to believe them!

Right now, choose to believe that the Bible is God's inerrant truth. Believe that He is your Heavenly Father Who loves you more than you can comprehend. Believe that all the exceedingly great and precious promises contained in His Word are for *you*. Believe that He wants to bless you with His miracle-working power.

Just *BELIEVE…*

CHAPTER THREE

YOUR MIRACLE *IS* GOD'S WILL

CAN YOU KNOW WITH CERTAINTY that it's God's will to perform a miracle in your life?

Well, what does the Bible say?

The Bible says that Jesus is the same yesterday, today, and forever (Hebrews 13:8). God says, *"I am the Lord. I change not!"* (Malachi 3:6 KJV)

We serve a God Who doesn't change. At the very beginning of creation, He miraculously spoke the universe into existence, and by His miracle-working power, He breathed life into man.

He performed mighty miracles for the children of Israel while they were in Egypt. Those miracles were so incredible that the news of them preceded the Israelites wherever they went. Hundreds of years later, the surrounding nations were still talking about them! (Joshua 9:9; 1 Samuel 4:7)

By His miraculous power, God divided the Red Sea. By His miraculous power He kept the Israelites alive in the wilderness for 40 years. Even their clothes and sandals didn't wear out (Nehemiah 9:21).

He tore down the walls of Jericho. He saved the lives of three Hebrew boys as they were thrown into a fiery furnace. He stopped the mouths of lions for Daniel in the lion's den. And these are just a few examples of God's miracle-working power!

But our great God is not just a Miracle Worker from the Old Testament. He still is the God of miracles and of the supernatural today!

Some Believers—and even many leaders in the Body of

Christ—say that God doesn't do miracles anymore...that miracles were just to prove Jesus' ministry while He was here on earth and to establish the apostles' leadership and authority for the early Church.

These same people generally believe that while we still have evangelists, pastors, and teachers, the days of the apostles, prophets, and miracles are over.

Well, I've personally experienced and witnessed many miracles, some of which I will share with you in this book, so I KNOW miracles ARE for today!

The Signs and Wonders of the Great Commission

To those who believe miracles went away when the last of the first apostles died, I'd like to ask them this:

Who did Jesus give the Great Commission to? Was His command to go into all the world and preach the Gospel given only to His disciples? And if He only gave the Great Commission to His disciples, then what's the point of us trying to reach people with the Gospel today?

Jesus *never* expected just those few men and women to reach the entire world!

And surely it makes sense that if the Great Commission was given not only to the disciples...not only to the early Church...but to the entire Body of Christ throughout all generations until Jesus returns, then *all* His words must be applicable for us today as well. He gave this command to *all* of His followers:

> *Go into all the world and preach the gospel to all creation. He who has believed and has been baptized shall be saved; but he who has disbelieved shall be condemned.*

> *These signs will accompany those who have believed:* in My name they will cast out demons, they will speak with new tongues; they will pick up serpents, and if they drink any deadly poison, it will not hurt them; they will lay hands on the sick, and they will recover.
>
> So then, when the Lord Jesus had spoken to them, He was received up into heaven and sat down at the right hand of God (Mark 16:15-19).

Who was Jesus addressing when He said, *"These signs will accompany those who have believed"*? Certainly it wasn't just the early disciples, since these words were said in the same breath that He gave the Great Commission.

God was, is, and always will be a God of MIRACLES! His nature cannot change. He doesn't manifest His miracle-working power one day and then go on vacation the next. Nowhere does the Bible say that these signs would only happen until those disciples died.

So how is it possible to arrive at the interpretation that Jesus only wanted His followers to perform miracles for the first 100 years after He was gone, or maybe the first 300 years, or even the first 1,000 years?

He told us to go into all the world and preach the Gospel and that signs will follow those who believe. *ALL OF US.*

What Does the *Bible* Say?

Part of the problem in the Church today is that we have pastors, leaders, and teachers who are coming up with their own interpretations of what the Bible says.

Jesus warned, *"This people honoureth me with their lips, but their heart is far from me. Howbeit in vain do they worship me, **teaching for doctrines the commandments of men**"* (Mark 7:6-7 KJV).

The apostle Paul also gave this warning found in 1 Timothy 1:6-7: *"For some men, straying from these things, have turned aside to fruitless discussion, wanting to be teachers of the Law, even though they do not understand either what they are saying or the matters about which they make confident assertions."*

In other words, people have come up with their own doctrines and beliefs...things they teach that are found—not in the Word of God—but in their own imaginations.

We need to ask ourselves, "What does the *Bible* say?"

Nowhere does the Bible describe a "day of miracles," as some have erroneously chosen to call the time when Jesus and the early apostles walked the earth. Nowhere in the Bible does it say that the authority Jesus delegated to His disciples and to those who later would believe and follow after Him would one day mysteriously disappear or simply stop happening.

We serve a God of miracle-working power Who is the same yesterday, today, and forever (Hebrews 13:8). He did not change His nature over the last 6,000 years. His nature and characteristics remain the same today as they were at the dawn of creation.

I agree with those theologians who say that there is no such thing as a "day of miracles." They're right...there isn't. There wasn't just a "day of miracles" 2,000 years ago or 4,000 years ago, and there isn't one today. There is simply a miracle-working, supernatural God, Who is still doing the same things today that He has done ever since He created the heavens and the earth and all that is in them.

I Believe!

God is supernatural, and He is to be worshipped as One Who has supernatural ability. He performed miracles, Jesus performed miracles, and the disciples performed miracles. Today, God is still backing up the authority of His children with His miracle-working power.

He intends for miracles to follow all those who believe in Jesus Christ as Lord and Savior. ALL Believers for all time are to exercise His supernatural authority.

There are several reasons why I believe in a God of miracle-working power:

1. The pattern of miracles is so clear throughout the Bible.
2. I've seen the miraculous take place before my very eyes as the lame walked, the blind were given sight, and the deaf could hear.
3. I've personally exercised the spiritual authority God has given me and seen Him back up that delegated authority with His miraculous power.
4. I've experienced firsthand the miraculous power of God in my life and in my family.

Let me share a testimony of a miracle that happened to me…

When I was a student at Oral Roberts University, I had a full-time job working for a company that had the food service contract on campus and provided all the student meals.

Eventually I was promoted to Student Manager. I was responsible for planning meals, ordering food, the hiring and firing of food service personnel, and creating the work schedules. Being a manager also meant working long hours.

I was working alone late one night, and because the dinner crew hadn't cleaned everything before leaving, I had to do it. I was in the kitchen cleaning a large meat cutter with big, circular, 12" diameter, razor-sharp blades.

As I was dismantling the meat cutter to clean it, I slipped and my forearm came down over the top of the blade. My arm instantly was slit open and began bleeding profusely.

I knew I was in major trouble. I immediately put my hand over the wound to put pressure on it in order to try and stop the bleeding. I was all by myself and bleeding all over the place, and all I can remember saying was, "Oh, Jesus!"

When I took my hand away to look at the wound, I discovered to my amazement that, although my arm was covered with blood, there was no cut!

I didn't know what to think. Had this really just happened to me? Was I only dreaming? There was my arm with no cut, but the blood was *everywhere*...on my arm, on the table, on the floor.

Even as I began cleaning up all the blood, I kept looking at my arm in disbelief. It was as though nothing had ever happened. Somehow, in that moment of simply calling on the name of Jesus, He had stepped into the immediate circumstance of my life in a miraculous way.

Was I expecting a miracle? Probably not. Was I doing all the things I'm sharing with you in this book? No. It was just a moment of great need in which I cried out to the Lord. And in that moment, He heard me, and He healed me!

So do I believe that miracles are for today? Absolutely!

Jesus Paid 100% of the Price!

Jesus came to set us free from sin, sickness, and death. Thank God that millions, and even billions, throughout the ages have been set free from sin and spiritual death.

But billions more have never been set free from sickness, loneliness, depression, anger, poverty, and so many other by-products of sin, the work of the flesh, and the power of Satan.

Jesus came to earth to pay 100% of the price for us to have 100% victory. He didn't come here and pay half the price for you, me, or anyone else.

The Word says He forgives ALL our sins (Psalm 103:3) and heals ALL our disease. How much is all? *ALL.* Not part, not some, not 50%. He forgives ALL our iniquities and heals ALL our diseases!

He purchased 100% of our healing with the stripes on

His back (Isaiah 53:5). One hundred percent of our tears will be wiped away and our sorrows will be taken away (Revelation 21:4).

Jesus paid a terrible price to make it possible for us to live in 100% spiritual, physical, and financial victory. Anything less is living below what our loving Heavenly Father wants for us as His kids.

If Jesus came to redeem us from the curse of sickness, then why do we live as though God wants us to go back and live underneath that curse?

If He doesn't want us to live under the curse of sin and death, why would He want us to live under the curse of sickness? Where do people get such twisted thinking that God *wants* us to be sick? He doesn't.

Never "If It Be Thy Will"!

"Lord, if it be Thy will." How many times have you heard someone pray that way? Maybe your pastor, your parents, or even you, have prayed these words. I believe that praying like this is a BIG mistake for a Believer.

The moment we interject the word "if," we're speaking words of doubt and uncertainty. "If" is a faith-killer. "If" says we don't know what to pray. "If" says we aren't sure of God's will. And a person who isn't sure that God wants to heal them probably isn't going to receive a healing miracle.

When you look in His Word, nowhere will you find that it's God's will for you to be sick, poor, destitute, lonely, depressed, confused, living in sin, or suffering any other curses or works of the devil. Nowhere will you find God say, "I wish you were miserable and destitute."

Do you want to know God's will? Then read the Bible, the Creator's "Owner's Manual" for His creation, where He clearly has revealed His will.

When we study God's Word, we KNOW His will for us: As our Heavenly Father Who loves us passionately, His heart's desire is to bless us even more than any earthly parent.

What do you want for *your* children? You want them to be healthy, happy, fulfilled, prosperous, and whole in body, mind, and spirit. So then what's God's will for *us*? The same!

"Or what man is there among you who, when his son asks for a loaf, will give him a stone? Or if he asks for a fish, he will not give him a snake, will he? If you then, being evil, know how to give good gifts to your children, how much more will your Father who is in heaven give what is good to those who ask him!" (Matthew 7:9-11)

How can we possibly pray, "Lord, if it is Your will, please heal my child," or "If it's Your will, please set my husband free from alcoholism." I *never* pray that way.

Are all of my prayers answered? No, of course not. I've had many prayers go unanswered. I'm not so foolish as to think that just because I believe something is His will that it's automatically going to happen when I think it should or in the way I think it should.

I've prayed for people who weren't healed and who eventually died. Do I believe it was God's will to heal them? Yes, absolutely. Then why weren't they miraculously healed? I don't know. But I can assure you that one day I'll find out why.

Regardless of what I may see with my natural eyes or fear in my own weak flesh, I refuse to use the word "if" when praying for God's will. Based on His Word, I *know* what His will is, and I'm going to keep praying it!

Where Are the Miracles?

Perhaps you're asking, "Well, if Jesus is such a Miracle-Worker, where are His miracles today?"

That's an important question.

First, let me say that God is still doing awesome miracles all over the world. I was privileged to grow up as the son of evangelist Morris Cerullo, a man of God who experiences tremendous healings in his crusades. So I've seen miracles all my life.

However, we have to face the fact that miracles are much too rare in the lives of most Christians today. We read about the powerful moves of the Holy Spirit in the book of Acts, but our own experience is quite different.

This shortage of miracles certainly isn't a result of any lack in God's ability or willingness to supernaturally intervene in the lives of His people. So why do we sometimes fail to see miraculous answers to our prayers? There could be many different reasons, but often the problem is simply an issue of our faith and obedience.

In Matthew 13, we read that when Jesus visited His hometown of Nazareth, *"He did not do many miracles there because of their unbelief"* (v. 58). Instead of receiving Jesus as the Messiah and Son of God, the townspeople asked, *"Is not this the carpenter's son?"* (v. 55).

How sad that people's lack of faith limited their ability to receive the miracles Jesus wanted to give them. Yet that's exactly the problem in the United States and in most Western nations today.

Professing Christians often go through the motions of praying and asking God for His miraculous intervention, but there is a serious shortage of genuine faith. As Paul warned, many people have *"a form of godliness, although they have denied its power"* (2 Timothy 3:5).

As I said earlier in this chapter, Jesus promised His disciples that miraculous signs would *"accompany those who have **believed**"* (Mark 16:17). Although we may ask, "Where are these signs today?" the real question is, "Where are these **Believers**?"

Jesus promised that whenever we truly believe in Him and lay hold of His supernatural power, **miracles are sure to fol-**

low. He opened the eyes of the blind, healed the lame, and raised the dead. And Jesus is the same yesterday, today and forever (Hebrews 13:8)!

I've said it before, and I will continue to proclaim it:

God said it. I believe it. That settles it. Let God be true and every man a liar (Romans 3:4)!

Believe!

An angel appeared to a young girl named Mary and told her that she would bear a child, even though she had never had a sexual experience with a man.

How would this be possible? And not only that, but the angel said this child would be called the Son of God, and He would save His people from their sins.

Let me ask you this: How in the world could Mary, a young teenage girl, have enough faith to make this happen? She didn't. She simply replied, *"Behold the handmaid of the Lord; be it unto me according to thy word"* (Luke 1:38).

I encourage you today...let child-like faith rise within you, and like Mary, believe the Word of the Lord.

BELIEVE!

CHAPTER FOUR
KEYS TO YOUR MIRACLE

LET'S PAUSE FOR A MOMENT NOW and consider this question: Exactly what *is* a miracle?

After all, if we're asking God for a miracle, we need to know what we're asking for! Here is a simple, but helpful, definition:

A MIRACLE IS AN EVENT OR ACTION THAT CONTRADICTS KNOWN NATURAL, SCIENTIFIC LAWS AND IS DUE TO A SUPERNATURAL CAUSE.

And what does "supernatural" mean?

This word comes from two words that have been put together: "super" (meaning "outside of") + "natural" (meaning "nature"). So...

AN EXPERIENCE IS CONSIDERED SUPERNATURAL WHEN IT HAPPENS OUTSIDE OF THE LAWS OF NATURE AND IS BEYOND THE NORMAL EXPERIENCE OR KNOWLEDGE OF MAN.

Since God is the Author, Creator, and Lord of the universe and all that is in it, He is the One Who established both natural and spiritual laws. It's only logical that He has control over these things and is not bound by the laws He Himself has created.

God is not limited by time or by space. He is sovereign and all-powerful. He has the ability to do anything He chooses.

Now that we've examined how to test sound Biblical doctrine in Chapter 2, let's look at just a few of the many supernatural events found throughout the Bible.

In each documented miracle in Scripture, there are exciting KEYS to discover…keys which you will want to possess in order to unlock YOUR miracle. These keys are powerful weapons of spiritual warfare you can use as you stand on the Lord's side to fight against the devil's strategies!

The Miracle of Jehoshaphat

The Bible says that even though Jehoshaphat's army numbered 1,160,000, there was such a great multitude coming against him that he was afraid. He knew for sure that without God's miraculous intervention, his army would be wiped out. Here's the story from 2 Chronicles 20:1-22 (KJV).

Miracle Key #1 – Set yourself to seek the Lord, and ask Him if He is calling you to fast for your miracle:

"It came to pass after this also, that the children of Moab, and the children of Ammon, and with them other beside the Ammonites, came against Jehoshaphat to battle. Then there came some that told Jehoshaphat, saying, There cometh a great multitude against thee from beyond the sea on this side Syria; and, behold, they be Hazazon-tamar, which is Engedi. And Jehoshaphat feared, and set himself to seek the LORD, and proclaimed a fast throughout all Judah" (vs. 1-3).

Miracle Key #2 – Recognize that you are calling on the LORD GOD, the powerful Ruler of the heavens and all the kingdoms of this world:

"And Judah gathered themselves together, to ask help of the LORD: even out of all the cities of Judah they came to seek the LORD. And Jehoshaphat stood in the congregation of Judah and Jerusalem, in the

house of the LORD, before the new court, and said,
'O LORD God of our fathers, art not thou God in
heaven? and rulest not thou over all the kingdoms of
the heathen? and in thine hand is there not power
and might, so that none is able to withstand thee?'"
(vs. 4-6)

Miracle Key #3 – Remember that God isn't just any "god"; He was the God of the children of Israel, and He is your God:

"Art not thou our God, who didst drive out the
inhabitants of this land before thy people Israel, and
gave it to the seed of Abraham thy friend forever?"
(v. 7)

Miracle Key #4 – Recognize that God has answered His children's prayers in times past with mighty miracles:

"And they [the Israelites] dwelt therein, and have
built thee a sanctuary therein for thy name, saying,
If, when evil cometh upon us, as the sword,
judgment, or pestilence, or famine, we stand before
this house, and in thy presence, (for thy name is in
this house,) and cry unto thee in our affliction, then
thou wilt hear and help" (vs. 8-9).

Miracle Key #5 – Don't rely on human strength or human wisdom for your miracle, but turn and focus your eyes on GOD:

"And now, behold, the children of Ammon and
Moab and mount Seir, whom thou wouldest not let
Israel invade, when they came out of the land of
Egypt, but they turned from them, and destroyed
them not; Behold, I say, how they reward us, to
come to cast us out of thy possession, which thou

hast given us to inherit. O our God, wilt thou not judge them? for we have no might against this great company that cometh against us; neither know we what to do: but our eyes are upon thee" (vs. 10-12).

Miracle Key #6 – Trust in God's Holy Spirit to guide you as you stand against fear, knowing that the battle for your miracle belongs to the LORD:

"And all Judah stood before the LORD, with their little ones, their wives, and their children. Then upon Jahaziel the son of Zechariah, the son of Benaiah, the son of Jeiel, the son of Mattaniah, a Levite of the sons of Asaph, came the Spirit of the LORD in the midst of the congregation; And he said, Hearken ye, all Judah, and ye inhabitants of Jerusalem, and thou king Jehoshaphat, Thus saith the LORD unto you, Be not afraid nor dismayed by reason of this great multitude; for the battle is not yours, but God's" (vs. 13-15).

Miracle Key #7 – Obey whatever God tells you to do, knowing that He is with you:

"Tomorrow go ye down against them: behold, they come up by the cliff of Ziz; and ye shall find them at the end of the brook, before the wilderness of Jeruel. Ye shall not need to fight in this battle: set yourselves, stand ye still, and see the salvation of the LORD with you, O Judah and Jerusalem: fear not, nor be dismayed; tomorrow go out against them: for the LORD will be with you" (vs. 16-17).

Miracle Key #8 – Worship God for giving you the miracle you need and praise Him *before* you see the victory:

"And Jehoshaphat bowed his head with his face to

the ground: and all Judah and the inhabitants of
Jerusalem fell before the LORD, worshipping the
LORD. And the Levites, of the children of the
Kohathites, and of the children of the Korhites, stood
up to praise the LORD God of Israel with a loud
voice on high" (vs. 18-19).

**Miracle Key #9 – Trust in God and those He has put in
your life to teach and lead you:**

*"And they rose early in the morning, and went forth
into the wilderness of Tekoa: and as they went forth,
Jehoshaphat stood and said, Hear me, O Judah, and
ye inhabitants of Jerusalem; Believe in the LORD
your God, so shall ye be established; believe his
prophets, so shall ye prosper"* (v. 20).

**Miracle Key #10 – Praise the Lord for His holiness and
mercy:**

*"And when he had consulted with the people, he
appointed singers unto the LORD, and that should
praise the beauty of holiness, as they went out before
the army, and to say, Praise the LORD; for his
mercy endureth for ever. And when they began to
sing and to praise, the LORD set ambushments
against the children of Ammon, Moab, and mount
Seir, which were come against Judah; and they were
smitten"* (vs. 21-22).

The Miracle of Naaman the Leper

Naaman was a man who needed a miraculous physical
healing, but first he had to die to his own idea of how this
should come about. His story is found in 2 Kings 5.

**Miracle Key #11 – Be prepared for God to speak to you
about your miracle through unexpected sources:**

"Now Naaman, captain of the army of the king of
Aram, was a great man with his master, and highly
respected, because by him the LORD had given victory
to Aram. The man was also a valiant warrior, but he
was a leper. Now the Arameans had gone out in bands
and had taken captive a little girl from the land of
Israel; and she waited on Naaman's wife. She said to
her mistress, 'I wish that my master were with the
prophet who is in Samaria! Then he would cure him
of his leprosy'" (vs. 1-3).

Miracle Key #12 – Always remember that God performs miracles to make HIS name great—not ours:

"Naaman went in and told his master, saying, 'Thus
and thus spoke the girl who is from the land of Israel.'
Then the king of Aram said, 'Go now, and I will send a
letter to the king of Israel.' He departed and took with
him ten talents of silver and six thousand shekels of
gold and ten changes of clothes. He brought the letter to
the king of Israel, saying, 'And now as this letter comes
to you, behold, I have sent Naaman my servant to you,
that you may cure him of his leprosy.' When the king of
Israel read the letter, he tore his clothes and said, 'Am I
God, to kill and to make alive, that this man is sending
word to me to cure a man of his leprosy? But consider
now, and see how he is seeking a quarrel against me.' It
happened when Elisha the man of God heard that the
king of Israel had torn his clothes, that he sent word to
the king, saying, 'Why have you torn your clothes? Now
let him come to me, and he shall know that there is a
prophet in Israel'" (vs. 4-8).

Miracle Key #13 – Don't let pride hinder your miracle. Humble yourself before the Lord and others:

*"So Naaman came with his horses and his chariots
and stood at the doorway of the house of Elisha.
Elisha sent a messenger to him, saying, 'Go and wash
in the Jordan seven times, and your flesh will be
restored to you and you will be clean.' But Naaman
was furious and went away and said, 'Behold, I
thought, "He will surely come out to me and stand
and call on the name of the LORD his God, and wave
his hand over the place and cure the leper." Are not
Abanah and Pharpar, the rivers of Damascus, better
than all the waters of Israel? Could I not wash in
them and be clean?' So he turned and went away in a
rage"* (vs. 9-12).

(NOTE: The River Jordan was a dirty river. Naaman
wanted to wash in the cleaner waters of Abanah and Pharpar.

There is a profound message here. Jordan means "River of
God," while Abanah means "manmade strength and security."
Pharpar stands for "man's ability to make clean, defeat, dis-
solve, divide, fail, frustrate, utterly make void."

Naaman wanted to do things *his* way, which was man's way.
The prophet was telling him to do things *God's* way, which was
to dip seven times in the river, God's number of perfection.)

Miracle Key #14 – Do things God's way, even when they may not make sense to you:

*"Then his servants came near and spoke to him and
said, 'My father, had the prophet told you to do some
great thing, would you not have done it? How much
more then, when he says to you, "Wash, and be
clean"?' So he went down and dipped himself seven
times in the Jordan, according to the word of the man
of God; and his flesh was restored like the flesh of a
little child and he was clean"* (vs. 13-14).

Miracle Key #15 – Give God all the glory when you receive your miracle:

"When he returned to the man of God with all his company, and came and stood before him, he said, 'Behold now, I know that there is no God in all the earth, but in Israel'" (v. 15).

The Miracle of Hezekiah

Sennacherib, King of Assyria, came up to war against Hezekiah, King of Judah. Hezekiah sought the Lord and prayed for God's miraculous intervention. Let's look at 2 Kings 19-20 and 2 Chronicles 32:24-26 to learn how God moved in this situation with His miracle-working power.

Miracle Key #16 – Declare that God is unlike false gods and that He alone is able to deliver you:

"Hezekiah prayed before the LORD and said, 'O LORD, the God of Israel, who are enthroned above the cherubim, You are the God, You alone, of all the kingdoms of the earth. You have made heaven and earth. Incline Your ear, O LORD, and hear; open Your eyes, O LORD, and see…now, O LORD our God, I pray, deliver us from his hand that all the kingdoms of the earth may know that You alone, O LORD, are God'" (19:15-19).

Miracle Key #17 – Even when your circumstances seem most desperate, "turn your face to the wall" and cry out to God with a broken spirit, reminding Him of His Covenant Relationship with His faithful children:

"In those days Hezekiah became mortally ill And Isaiah the prophet the son of Amoz came to him and

40

*said to him, 'Thus says the LORD, "Set your house in
order, for you shall die and not live." Then he turned
his face to the wall and prayed to the LORD, saying,
'Remember now, O LORD, I beseech You, how I have
walked before You in truth and with a whole heart
and have done what is good in Your sight.' And
Hezekiah wept bitterly"* (20:1-3).

Miracle Key #18 – Trust that the Lord loves you, hears your prayers, and sees your tears:

*"Before Isaiah had gone out of the middle court, the
word of the LORD came to him, saying, 'Return and
say to Hezekiah the leader of My people, "Thus says
the LORD, the God of your father David, 'I have
heard your prayer, I have seen your tears; behold, I
will heal you. On the third day you shall go up to the
house of the LORD'"""* (vs. 4-5).

Miracle Key #19 – After receiving your miracle, remain humble and grateful before the Lord:

*"In those days Hezekiah became mortally ill; and he
prayed to the LORD, and the LORD spoke to him and
gave him a sign. But Hezekiah gave no return for the
benefit he received, because his heart was proud;
therefore wrath came on him and on Judah and
Jerusalem. However, Hezekiah humbled the pride of
his heart, both he and the inhabitants of Jerusalem, so
that the wrath of the LORD did not come on them in
the days of Hezekiah"* (2 Chronicles 32:24-26).

The Miracle of Blind Bartimaeus

In Mark 10, we read the story of Bartimaeus, a blind man
who was living out his life begging by the side of the road. He

was in such a pitiful state that he knew his only hope rested in the mercy and miracle-working power of Jesus Christ.

By faith, Bartimaeus was willing to cry out persistently for his miracle, regardless of what others said or thought about him.

Miracle Key #20 – Don't be ashamed to cry out for Jesus to help and heal you:

"Then they came to Jericho. And as He was leaving Jericho with His disciples and a large crowd, a blind beggar named Bartimaeus, the son of Timaeus, was sitting by the road. When he heard that it was Jesus the Nazarene, he began to cry out and say, 'Jesus, Son of David, have mercy on me!'" (vs. 46-47)

Miracle Key #21 – Be persistent, refusing to be silenced or embarrassed by the opinions and thoughts of others:

"Many were sternly telling him to be quiet, but he kept crying out all the more, 'Son of David, have mercy on me!'" (v. 48)

Miracle Key #22 – Don't be afraid to be specific and tell Jesus exactly what you are asking Him to do for you, knowing that faith results in miracles:

"And Jesus stopped and said, 'Call him here.' So they called the blind man, saying to him, 'Take courage, stand up! He is calling for you.' Throwing aside his cloak, he jumped up and came to Jesus. And answering him, Jesus said, 'What do you want Me to do for you?' And the blind man said to Him, 'Rabboni, I want to regain my sight!' And Jesus said to him, 'Go; your faith has made you well.' Immediately he regained his sight and began following Him on the road" (vs. 49-52).

The Miracle of the Woman with the Issue of Blood

Because large crowds often followed Jesus and pressed in on Him from every side, He could be hard to get close to. How could anyone, let alone a sick woman, weakened by loss of blood for 12 years make her way through the large crowd to talk to Him or touch Him?

It would take determination! Let's read her faith-building story in Mark 5.

Miracle Key #23 – Understand that while medical science is a valuable tool in God's hand, doctors do not have all the answers, and they are not the final word:

"And a large crowd was following Him and pressing in on Him. A woman who had had a hemorrhage for twelve years, and had endured much at the hands of many physicians, and had spent all that she had and was not helped at all, but rather had grown worse" (vs. 25-26).

Miracle Key #24 – Grab hold of the truth that Jesus can and will heal you; then act on that belief by grabbing hold of Him with faith and determination:

"After hearing about Jesus, she came up in the crowd behind Him and touched His cloak. For she thought, 'If I just touch His garments, I will get well.' Immediately the flow of her blood was dried up; and she felt in her body that she was healed of her affliction" (vs. 27-29).

Miracle Key #25 – As you receive your miracle from the Lord Jesus, Who has such compassion on you, know that your faith in Him results in the release of His power into your life:

"Immediately Jesus, perceiving in Himself that the power proceeding from Him had gone forth, turned around in the crowd and said, 'Who touched My garments?' And His disciples said to Him, 'You see the crowd pressing in on You, and You say, "Who touched Me?"' And He looked around to see the woman who had done this. But the woman fearing and trembling, aware of what had happened to her, came and fell down before Him and told Him the whole truth. And He said to her, 'Daughter, your faith has made you well; go in peace and be healed of your affliction'" (vs. 30-34).

My friend, the Bible is packed full of miraculous stories. God's Word is our authority, and because He loves us, He has given us these stories as examples to teach us about His miracle-working power:

"Now these things happened to them as an example, and they were written for our instruction, upon whom the ends of the ages have come" (1 Corinthians 10:10-11).

I encourage you to read His Word and discover for yourself the Miracle Keys it holds to help you unlock the doors leading to *your* miracle.

God Is Faithful!

Throughout the years, Barbara and I have used these Miracle Keys and have been blessed by God's wonder-working power in our life and family. Just one of our many personal testimonies to God's miracles is about our son Ben.

Ben was 18 years old when he decided to leave. He hadn't run away—he had just moved away from home. But not only was he away from home…he was away from God.

Many were the nights when Barb and I would venture into Ben's bedroom to kneel by his empty bed and pray.

Time and again, we would use these different Miracle Keys,remembering…declaring…weeping…praying…praising …persisting…and trusting the Lord to answer our prayers and bring Ben home to us and back to Himself.

Years passed, and nothing in the natural world seemed to be happening. But then we began to see God's miracle answers come in stages.

First, Ben came home on his own, and soon, he came "home" to the Lord. Next, he married our lovely daughter-in-law Jessica, and then Ben responded to the Holy Spirit's promptings to begin a powerful youth ministry.

In a national Christian magazine, Ben was recently named one of the 30 most influential youth leaders in the United States!

During those desperate nights spent crying out to God in an empty room by an empty bed, we never considered that such an honor was even remotely possible. But those years of praying, believing, and praising have been rewarded and blessed by God's mercy and His miracle-working power.

What we endured has become part of our testimony to the importance of perseverance and the faithfulness of God.

Be encouraged today…God hasn't forgotten you or your need. ***He is faithful!***

CHAPTER FIVE

GOD CAN DO IT FOR YOU!

I'VE BEEN PRIVILEGED TO PERSONALLY witness people being healed by the miraculous power of God as the devil's power is broken.

More than once in my life, I have confronted demonic powers in people who were possessed. When they opened their mouth, their lips didn't move, and their tongue didn't move, but a voice came out. I've seen those people delivered by God's power through faith in the name of Jesus.

It overwhelms me every time I witness a miracle or hear a testimony of God's miraculous intervention in someone's life. His freedom always puts smiles on faces and fills heart with joy. We can't help but rejoice and thank God for His miracles!

We must always remember that it's never a person who does the healing. *God* does the healing. However, while it's His power, He requires *us* to exercise the authority He's given us through Jesus Christ to heal the sick, cast out demons, and overcome the works of the devil.

His Ability, Our Obedience

I don't believe things happen on earth without us. God has chosen to work through His children. He isn't concerned about our abilities, how much Scripture we can quote, or how perfectly we pray.

It's *His* ability that matters, not ours. However, He *is*

concerned about our obedience. God rules through His spoken Word and so must we!

You'll never see the miraculous take place in your life—and you'll never rule your world with the authority God has given you—until you learn the power of your words.

As we have learned to live and walk in this truth, Barbara and I have seen God move miraculously in our family, finances, and health.

Seeing the miraculous hand of God at work is what has helped me to know that God is real and that His wonder-working power is real. I can't deny Him or what I've seen.

The very first miracles I remember were when I was a little boy sitting on the front row of my dad's crusades. He would have healing lines, and people would come forward to be prayed for one by one.

I'll never forget the first time I saw people healed whose one leg was significantly shorter than the other. They would sit in a chair with both legs up on another chair, and then, without anyone even touching them, the power of God would come on them, their short leg would begin to quiver and shake, and then, on its own, grow out to match the length of the other leg!

"They're Expecting To Be Prayed For!"

I've also been blessed to see God move in miraculous ways in response to my own prayers, with sick people healed, the deaf given their hearing, and the lame able to walk.

The very first miracle I remember God working through me in obedience to Him was when I prayed for a woman while preaching at a crusade service in Toronto, Canada.

Actually, it wasn't even my meeting. I was a teenager, and the last thing I felt called to do was preach the Gospel. It was Dad's crusade, but he had been called home to San Diego on an emergency.

He could have asked one of the pastors to preach, or he could have asked the crusade chairman to bring the message. So I was stunned when Dad asked *me* to lead the service. I was only 16 years old or so, and I was petrified! I had never done anything like that before.

Well, I spent the day in my motel room praying and asking the Lord what He wanted me to say. That night, I shared the message the Lord had put in my heart, and when I gave an altar call, people came forward to be saved. I led them in the "Sinner's Prayer," and then I sat down.

The crusade chairman came to me and said, "Your dad prays for the sick, and these people have come expecting to be prayed for." There I was, a 16-year-old kid, and I didn't know what to do.

But I stood up in the pulpit again and asked anyone who was sick and needed prayer to come forward. I formed them into a line, and then I went down the line, laying hands on each one and praying for them.

I don't remember everything God did that night, but I do remember one woman in particular, who burst into tears after I prayed for her.

The smile on her face was full of joy, and she couldn't stop saying, "I can hear! I can hear! I can hear!" When I asked her what was happening, she told me that she didn't have an eardrum in that ear and had never been able to hear out of it. Yet there she was, hearing out of an ear with no eardrum! God touched her, and as He did, her hands were lifted to Him in praise and thanksgiving.

God wasn't depending on me or my 16-year-old abilities. He was depending on Himself and His Word. But because I was obedient to use the *authority* He had given me, He backed up that authority with His miracle-working power. Yes, even coming from the mouth of a 16-year-old youth, God stands behind the authority He has delegated to us!

He Can Do It for YOU!

God's Word is packed with supernatural stories of how He delights in stepping into the circumstances of His children's lives to bring victory, healing, and deliverance. And through my experience, the Biblical truth of miracles became a part of my very being when I was just a boy.

Because I learned firsthand that God is a God of miracle-working power, there is nothing anyone can ever do or say to convince me that God isn't real or that He isn't Who the Bible says He is.

I've seen it. I've experienced it. I believe it.

Testimonies are powerful proof that God is performing miracles in people's lives today. What God has done for someone else, He can surely do for you!

Here are some stories of people who have experienced miracles through Inspiration Ministries. These are just a few of the many thousands of letters Barbara and I receive each year from Partners who are praising God for stepping into the circumstances of their lives with His miracle-working power.

"I Was Addicted to Crystal Methamphetamine"

"I want to share how a broadcast from INSP changed my life. For 13 years I was addicted to alcohol and crystal methamphetamine. It was really taking a toll on my wife and three children.

"One night at 1:00 a.m., I came home from getting high and turned on your campmeeting. The minister said that God would command an anointing on my life and that I would never be the same. Without hesitating, I called in an offering of $240. Then I left and went back to my friend's home. When I got back home again, I turned on INSP, and this time I woke my wife to watch with me.

"Within the next 10 days, I was caught up into God's Presence. From that night on, I have been completely clean and sober and sharing my testimony at church conferences.

"Not long after this, I was terminated from my job. Eight months later I received a settlement from the company that had terminated me for $24,000—that's a 100-fold return on my original gift to the Lord.

"I have since been studying for the ministry and hope to be ordained in a few months. God has also provided a new job for me with a Christian-owned company. David and Barbara, I hope and pray that my story will bring joy to your day. Your ministry has turned my life around. May God continue to bless the work of your hands."—*S.H.*

"Jesus Has Given Me a Wonderful Miracle"

"Last year my doctors told me that I had a cancerous cyst growing in my female organs. Several sets of x-rays and two biopsies confirmed their diagnosis—the large mass was definitely malignant. My family and I received this news with great dread. You see, four of my sisters had all died of cancer. At age 70, I could see how this disease had taken an unusually high claim on my family.

"I'm an Inspiration Partner with David and Barbara, so I knew I needed to call their prayer ministry for help. Following our time of prayer, I went to see my doctors again. They wanted to complete final testing and discuss a course of treatment with me. But the large mass they'd found had disappeared. The Lord Jesus had given me a wonderful Miracle, and today I am healed!"—*O.H.*

"My Eyes Were Instantly Healed!"

"I have lived by my faith in Jesus for many, many years. I see that so often we Christians settle for crumbs from God's table when He wants us to share in His feast.

"My younger life was very difficult. I suffered from both

rheumatic fever and neuritis so that my body was nearly paralyzed. But one night at a tent meeting, a preacher spoke God's Word over me and the glory fell. I was instantly healed! For the first time in my life, I was able to get a job and take care of myself.

"David, one day when you were sharing about the City of Light, you said you would send us each a little piece of that land. You weren't claiming that the soil had any miracle powers or anything like that.

"But while reading your wonderful letter, I noticed that my packet of soil began to burn in my hand. Then the Holy Spirit told me to place that packet over each of my eyes.

"You see, four months ago some landscapers had sprayed chemicals on the lawns, and it had gotten in my eyes. They had been watering, itching, and swelling up ever since. It was a miserable feeling.

"But as soon as I obeyed the Lord and placed your packet of soil over my eyes, they were instantly healed! From that moment on, I have not had any problems. Also, a sty I'd had for days just disappeared the next morning!

"I am sensing there will one day be many, many healings at the City of Light!"—*V.H.*

"We Saw a 7-Fold Return!"

"We live in Port Arthur, Texas, where Hurricane Rita devastated our town. At that time, all our residents evacuated to a town called Gladewater.

"My husband, Keith, and I were living temporarily in a motel there. We'd never heard of Inspiration Ministries before, but we found you on the cable TV in our room.

"The Red Cross and FEMA (Federal Emergency Management Agency) had together given each refugee family $1000 assistance. We then heard on the news that our home town had been destroyed by the storm.

"We knew we would need a lot more than $1000 to get our lives back together if all the reports were true. So we mailed the $1000 to your ministry for Souls that very day.

"Our town of Port Arthur would never be the same. Many homes and businesses were totally destroyed, and a lot of people just gave up and moved away. However, on returning, we were amazed to find that our own home was one of the few not terribly damaged by the storm! In fact, we only had minimal work to do before living there. Praise God!

"Within the next few months, money was sent to us from many sources so that we saw a seven-fold return on our $1000 offering. This was a wonderful blessing since the insurance company, being so overwhelmed with claims, didn't send us anything for another three months. All glory be to Jesus, and may He bless The Inspiration Networks in every way!"—*K.L.*

"I Have No More Pain"

"Twenty years ago I was servicing an elevator when I fell into the shaft. My spine was severely injured with several of my vertebrae badly displaced. Even with all my medical treatment, for nearly a year my back was basically numb from injury to the nerves. When the numbness finally left, I found myself in continual pain.

"Last spring, my wife Muriel and I were watching The Inspiration Networks' campmeeting, and the speaker began leading the audience in prayer. Then my wife did something we had not done before. She stood up there in the living room and raised her hands in agreement, worshiping God. I decided to join her.

"Incredibly, once I had raised my hands in worship to Jesus, I began feeling and hearing a strange 'crackling' sound in my back. Then, when I lowered my arms again, I realized that all my back pain had totally left me. For the first time in 20 years, I was pain free!

"We were so overwhelmed by this great miracle from God that I immediately wanted to give thanks. I sat down and wrote the largest check I have ever written to any organization ($2000) and sent it to your ministry.

"I have no more pain, and now I can lift anything I want! We praise Jesus and express our deep thanks to David and Barbara Cerullo for this wonderful ministry that opened our hearts to God's Miracle-Working Power!"—*L.S.*

"He Hasn't Drunk a Drop"

"My husband Nicholas was an alcoholic for 40 of our married years. I prayed continuously for him to be saved. One day about 20 years ago, I had a vision of Nicholas walking down the center aisle of our church with his hands raised in surrender to the Lord. This was very personal between the Lord and me, so I never told anyone.

"This past year, I learned on Inspiration Ministries how we can give our offerings to God while asking Him for a Miracle in our lives. So I decided to give an offering and ask for the soul of my husband.

"Well, one Sunday, I was at church just before the service, and I had stepped into the back to get something. Suddenly, my friend came running to me, saying, 'Geneva, your husband is walking down the sidewalk toward the church!' I couldn't believe it.

"I hurried back inside the church and there was Nicholas, walking down the center aisle of the church, his hands in the air, saying, 'I don't want to go to hell. Jesus, save me!' Nicholas got all the way to the altar where he gave his soul to Jesus. And he hasn't drunk a drop since then.

"Nicholas is now a true servant of the Lord. He helps at the church, and he is one of the finest Christians I know. I thank God for hearing the prayers of my heart and honoring my gift of faith. Praise the Lord. He made my vision a reality!"—*G.L.*

"God Spared Our Lives"

"My wife Pauline and I drive a tractor trailer. This past summer, we were carrying a full load of meat packing materials to Guymon, Oklahoma. The weather had gotten very bad, but truck drivers get used to handling tough road conditions. Suddenly, we were hit by very high winds. I realized too late that we had run right into the deadliest storm on earth—a tornado! I struggled to keep control of my truck, but we jackknifed and began sliding toward the overhang. I yelled to Pauline that we were going over the side!

"We immediately began praising God, calling out the name of Jesus, and proclaiming His glory. We then experienced the most wonderful Miracle! The truck stopped sliding and was lifted about a foot off the road. I couldn't turn the steering wheel, and we were still jackknifed. But the whole truck was suddenly being carried in the air in the direction we had been driving!

"Neither of us could believe our eyes. The lines in the road moved beneath us as we kept going forward. This was totally impossible, but it was happening! Eventually, the truck gently set back down, and I was able to turn the steering wheel again. We then drove on into Guymon.

"We knew our story was so amazing that it would be hard for anyone to believe. But it happened! We thank God for His goodness in sparing our lives that day. And we thank The Inspiration Networks for the great programs that inspire faith for wonderful Miracles in the lives of everyone."—J.S.

"I Give God the Glory!"

"I called your Prayer Center because I suffered so greatly from migraine headaches. Some of these would last for five consecutive days without letting up. Then after they stopped, I often would have to endure a rebound headache.

"But after your prayer minister interceded with me, I immediately stopped taking my medication. I'm a nurse, so I knew you're not supposed to stop this particular medication all at once. But the Lord released me to do just that, and I've never taken it again. I rarely have any headaches since that night. This all happened two years ago, and I give God the glory!"—D.G.

"My Husband Received a Check for $15,000!"

"My husband is a 100% disabled military veteran. We had been trying to get the government to release his pension or disability funds for a long, long time with no results. This created a terrible financial hardship for our family.

"Then I heard on Inspiration Ministries that God releases His blessings if we approach Him in faith. So we sent in our offering in hopes that He would miraculously intervene on our behalf.

"Six weeks later, my husband received a check for $15,000 in back pension pay! The next week, he received an additional check for $21,000. Then, the government notified us that we qualified for an $11,000 grant toward a new handicap-equipped van.

"Thank you so much for teaching us how our faith can move God's hand for the Miraculous!"—K.M.

"We Had a Resurrection From the Dead!"

"As promised, please find enclosed three checks for my offering. I had called you with an urgent request for prayer for my niece who had taken a massive drug overdose. Her father (my brother) drove seven hours overnight to get to her.

"The day after I phoned you, he was with her at the hospital when her heart stopped. It seemed we had lost her, and the doctors were preparing to take her off life support.

"But then my brother said to her in faith, 'Julie, open your eyes.' There was no reaction. Then he said, 'Julie, it's your dad speaking. Now open your eyes.' Her eyes opened. Hallelujah! We had a resurrection from the dead!

"Julie is doing well now. We even received a nice card from her recently. Thank you! I know that, as we sought the Throne of God together, He answered my family's cry for a mighty Miracle."—*S.D.*

"God Has Done a Miracle for Me!"

"My husband was a witch doctor chief in our tribe in Cameroon, Africa. He kept a pet anaconda snake in our house, and he worshiped it as his ancestral spirit.

"I lived for years in abuse and ill health as spells and curses filled our home. My body was always in pain, and I never knew why. Then, one day, a missionary visiting a nearby village led me to Jesus Christ. I was so happy!

"But when my husband learned of it, he began beating me every night. In the dark, when I would secretly kneel in my room to pray, his snake would slither in and try to attack me. It was so terrifying!

"So I ran away and came to the U.S. Yet still my body endured many unknown pains and afflictions. And every night, I would have nightmares that his serpent was coming here to destroy me.

"When I discovered Inspiration Ministries on TV, I called in, and a lady prayed for me. Suddenly, all the pain I had suffered for years left my body. God had done a Miracle for me! The evil nightmares are gone, and now my Christian faith is growing as never before! I am thankful that I am free from that curse of voodoo forever."—*S.F.*

"My Husband Received Jesus!"

"Three months after sending my first offering to your ministry, my husband received Jesus into his life after I had been praying for him for 23 years! He would never listen to a word I had to say about God, but now he is saved, baptized in the Holy Spirit, and a completely changed person.

"God has worked a mighty Miracle in our lives. My husband has been saved exactly six months today as I write this letter, and they have been the most wonderful six months of the last 35 years.

"I am totally convinced that this Miracle is the result of Sowing Seed into the Good Ground of Inspiration Ministries. Praise God. May your ministry continue to be blessed of God always."—K.A.

"God Took a Tragedy and Turned It Into a Wonderful Gift of Life!"

"My wife, Jeana, was pregnant with our third child and everything seemed to be going well. She was healthy, and we already had two small children, so we didn't expect any surprises this time.

"Then one day, the baby inside her just stopped moving, so we rushed Jeana to the hospital. Her obstetrician diagnosed that our unborn baby had suffered a stroke. This was very serious, for it meant that our little girl was bleeding inside her brain.

"A level 4 stroke like this one almost always means the child will be born dead or, at the least, have severe brain damage, mental retardation, blindness, or cerebral palsy.

"As a physician myself, I fully understood the danger we faced. This condition is so rare that it happens in less than one in a million births. The cause is unknown.

"My wife and I are believers in God's power to heal and to deliver, so we called all our friends and asked for prayer. My grandmother is an Inspiration Partner with Inspiration Ministries, and she phoned your prayer ministry in our time of desperation.

"Twelve hours after we heard the terrible news, our baby was delivered through caesarean section. That was almost two years ago.

"I praise the Lord that our little girl, Olivia Jean, is now walking and talking and very healthy. She has developed normally and shows no signs of the stroke that nearly took her life.

"We give glory to the Lord Jesus for hearing our prayers and those of all our friends. He took a tragedy and turned it into a wonderful gift of life!"—*Dr. R.R.*

"My Beloved Son Appeared in My Doorway!"

"Over 20 years ago, my son experienced a terrible tragedy when his own 13-year-old boy was tragically killed in a farming accident. For my dear son, the shock of this loss was unbearable.

"After that, he withdrew from nearly everyone and would have no contact with anyone, not even me. Even though we lived in the same city, I never saw or heard from him.

"I tried for so long to reach out, but I found that some grief is so deep, human love simply cannot touch it. So I finally gave it all up to Jesus. I gave the Lord a special offering through your ministry, asking Him to do what I could not do.

"Amazingly, only a few weeks later, my beloved son appeared in my doorway! He shared how his life had just fallen apart after his boy died and that he had just wanted to be away from everyone, even the people he loved.

"Since that day, my beloved son comes here often, and we have a beautiful relationship. I have to thank the Lord for His mercy, for answering my prayers after so many years, and for His Miracle healing in my family."—*P.H.*

"He Has Totally Changed My Life!"

"My life was a shattered mess five years ago. Drug addiction had cost me everything and almost my life. Lying on my cot in a jail cell, I listened as my attorney stated that I was facing 99 years in prison!

"It was this time of terrible pressure that God used to break the chains that had me bound. I began asking Him for direction. Inspiration Ministries was a great source of hope and comfort to me in those dark days. In faith, I began sending my offerings to your ministry, hoping that somehow God would send a Miracle my way.

"Well, He has totally changed my life. I'm now out of prison, and today I am 55 years old with a beautiful family God has given me to love. Four weeks ago a friend set me up with an interview, and I was given a job paying three times what I made before. I even got my home back that I had lost during my trial. I could go on and on about the Miracles God has given me time and time again over the past five years."—S.L.

"I Knew I Could Be Imprisoned or Severely Beaten"

"I am a Christian living in the Muslim nation of Saudi Arabia. Your television ministry helps me learn to believe God's Word in everything.

"Last night, I was transacting business with a local bank, and I was trying to send a bank draft to your ministry. Suddenly, I was taken into custody by the bank guards and interrogated on the purpose of my sending money to David Cerullo.

"I responded that it was my personal support to this TV network but refrained from telling them that it's all about God's Kingdom, fearing that I might be taken away for further interrogation.

"In my country, it is against the law to send money to Christian organizations. I knew I could be imprisoned or severely beaten. Some Christians have even been killed for their faith here.

"So I prayed to God to take away the fear I felt at that moment and, likewise, for the Holy Spirit to speak to those two bank officers who had been holding me for some time.

"Then, suddenly, the same bank officer called me in and personally handed me the bank draft! I am sending it with this letter.

"I thank and praise God through the Lord Jesus Christ for that experience. I see that in every trying moment in a Christian's life, God is always there beside us."—A.C.

Jesus Is Carrying You Through

Aren't these powerful and encouraging testimonies? Doesn't it thrill your heart and give you hope that if God performed His miracle-working power for these folks, He can do it for you, too?

But what about the times when we don't see God at work in our lives? Those times when we wonder if He is there, if He still hears our prayers, or if He even loves us?

Friend, realize that He was there…He *is* there…*all* the time…carrying you through those difficult circumstances in ways you cannot see.

I'm reminded of the story of the person who was looking back over his life, and the Lord showed him two sets of footprints along the sandy shoreline. But from time-to-time, there would be only one set.

"Lord," he asked, "Where were You during those times when I was walking alone?"

The Lord answered, "I was there, My precious child. It was then that I was carrying you."

I'm praying for Jesus to use these encouraging, miraculous testimonies to "carry you" through to the miracle breakthrough *you* need.

CHAPTER SIX

EXPECT YOUR MIRACLE

IN THIS CHAPTER, I WANT TO BUILD your faith to expect a miracle from God. Not hope for one. Not wish for one. *EXPECT ONE.*

When a gardener plants a garden, she spends a long time turning the soil, adding nutrients, planting the seeds at the right depth, watering the seeds, and pulling out weeds.

She isn't working long and hard preparing that garden and sowing seeds just for fun. While she may enjoy the process, she's investing her time, effort, and resources because she has an expectation. She is sowing those seeds for a desired result...harvest!

My dad taught me many years ago always to look for parallels between the natural realm and the spiritual world because God uses the natural to teach us about the spiritual (1 Corinthians 15:46).

It's easy to see how sowing seeds to reap a harvest in a garden is like Sowing Seeds to Reap a Harvest in our spiritual lives. In the natural, we plant seeds for a desired result: We want to reap a harvest.

It's the same in the spiritual realm.

Sowing and Reaping

Sometimes people say to me, "But David, *I* don't give in order to get." You know, I just don't understand that kind of thinking. Of *course* we give to get...

Do we Sow Seeds of respect to others and expect to be treated with respect in return? Certainly.

Do we Sow Seeds of love into our families and hope to Reap a Harvest of love in return? Absolutely.

Do we Sow our time and skill into our jobs and want to Reap a paycheck at the end of the week? Definitely.

So *do* we Sow Seeds to Reap a particular Harvest? All the time.

Consider our tithes and offerings to the Lord. We give these to Him, trusting in His promise to abundantly bless our obedience and rebuke the devourer:

> *"Bring the whole tithe into the storehouse, so that there may be food in My house, and test Me now in this,' says the LORD of hosts, 'if I will not open for you the windows of heaven and pour out for you a blessing until it overflows.*
>
> *'Then I will rebuke the devourer for you, so that it will not destroy the fruits of the ground; nor will your vine in the field cast its grapes,' says the LORD of hosts. 'All the nations will call you blessed, for you shall be a delightful land,' says the LORD of hosts"* (Malachi 3:10-12).

To those who say, "I don't give to get," I say be prepared, because God's Word is clear: When we Sow, we *will* Reap a Harvest:

> *"Do not be deceived, God is not mocked; for whatever a man sows, this he will also reap. For the one who sows to his own flesh will from the flesh reap corruption, but the one who sows to the Spirit will from the Spirit reap eternal life"* (Galatians 6:7-8).

If you don't expect to Reap when you have Sown, then you

most likely either won't receive your Harvest, or you'll miss it when it comes because you won't be looking for it.

When You Have a Miracle Need, Sow a Miracle Seed

Do you need a miracle? Then Sow a Seed! What is a "Seed"? Your Seed is…

* A tiny beginning that can become more.
* Something you give away to produce what you've been promised.
* Your bridge to your future.

In nature, every seed contains DNA—an invisible set of instructions for what it will be. An acorn becomes an oak tree. An apple seed produces apples. A father's seed produces a child.

The same is true in the spiritual realm. The spiritual Seeds we Sow into God's Kingdom have a spiritual DNA that will determine the Harvest it will become. A Seed can be…

* Prayer	* Forgiveness
* Kindness	* Joy
* Love	* Gratitude
* Time	* Hope
* Patience	* Faith
* Money	* Humor
* Thoughts	* Help
* Talents	* Peace

But just as it takes time to reap a harvest in nature, it also takes time for our spiritual Seeds to Reap a Harvest. No one goes out into a garden today, plants seeds, and then returns tomorrow to gather up a bouquet of flowers or pick vegetables to make a salad.

In the same way, we need to wait long enough for our spiritual Seeds to produce the Harvests we desire. Waiting reveals our trust. While we're waiting, we must water our precious Seeds with our love and worship, obedience to God and His Word, and an attitude of belief, expectancy, and thanksgiving.

Release the Seed in Your Hand

We must learn to Sow Seed consistently. Farmers know that continuous planting brings continuous crops. They also know that the reverse is also true: uneven sowing yields uneven harvests.

It's no different when we're Sowing Seeds into God's Kingdom. Continuous Sowing results in continuous Reaping.

It's also important to Sow in proportion to the miracle Harvest we need, because the size of our Seed determines the size of our Harvest.

If a gardener only wants a flower in a pot, then she only plants a few seeds. But if she wants an abundant garden full of beautiful flowers and delicious vegetables, then she had better plant plenty of Seeds!

Do you want your Harvest to increase? Then increase the size of your Seed. If your Seed is precious to you and costs you something, it will be precious to God. But if your Seed isn't important to you, then it won't be important to God either.

Keep in mind, too, that when we just hold on to the Seeds God has given us, then Seed is also our Harvest. On the other hand, when we release our Seed by Sowing it with faith into God's Kingdom, we can expect to Reap His Harvest. When we release the Seed in *our* hands, God releases the Harvest in *His* hands.

The quality of the soil into which we Sow is another key factor in determining our Harvest. According to the Word, some Harvests are going to yield a 30-fold return, some 60, and some will yield a 100-fold increase, depending on whether or not the Seeds are Sown into *"good ground"* (Matthew 13:8).

A Financial Miracle Testimony

What miracle are you seeking from God today?

Is it for a financial breakthrough? Let me tell you about a financial miracle that Barb and I experienced early in our marriage after we Sowed a financial Seed.

We were in our first year of marriage, and we heard an appeal. We sensed the Holy Spirit speaking to us and leading us to give an offering.

I looked at Barbara, and she looked at me and said to me, "Are you feeling like we are supposed to give an offering?"

I said, "Yes, I am."

She said, "You tell me, and then I'll tell you the amount I'm thinking of."

We were both feeling led to give $300, which also happened to be every last penny we had in savings—a lot for two kids who were just married and recently out of college. But that's all we had, and we gave it all!

A few weeks later, I received a letter in the mail from a woman, and although I didn't save it (I wish I had!), her letter went something like this...

> *"Dear David,*
>
> *You don't know who I am. I don't really know who you are. But I was in prayer and the Lord dropped your name into my heart and said I was supposed to write you and send you this. I am sure that you will know what it is for, because this is what God told me to do."*

I opened the letter, and there was $700!

Remember when I talked about how in the natural, a gardener sows seeds because she expects to reap a harvest from those seeds? And do you remember that I told you how this principle of Sowing and Reaping applies to both the natural realm and the spiritual realm?

I encourage you to plant a Seed for your miracle right now. As you do, know that I am standing in prayer in agreement with you for God to move on your behalf and release the miracle you need into your life.

Seeds of Expectation

There are many stories in the Bible of people who Sowed precious Seed in order to receive a specific, desired Harvest.

For example, the first thing Noah did when he got off the ark was to "Sow a Seed" by giving a sacrificial offering to the Lord. It was *after* the Lord smelled the sacrifice that He promised to never again destroy every living thing. In fact, it's in this same story that God established His eternal Covenant of Seedtime and Harvest (Genesis 8:21-22).

King David is another example. When God sent an angel to destroy Jerusalem, David Sowed a Seed to stop the hand of the destroyer. When God saw David's Seed, He told the angel to hold back (1 Chronicles 21:26-27).

In 1 Kings 17, there's another great story about Sowing and Reaping. Let's take a closer look at it…

There was a widow who was living during a time of great famine. She had just enough flour left in her bowl and oil in her jar to make a cake for herself and her son, and then she was assuming that they both were going to die from starvation. But God sent a prophet to her home with a miraculous plan:

> *Then the word of the LORD came to him, saying,*
> *'Arise, go to Zarephath, which belongs to Sidon, and*

*stay there; behold, I have commanded a widow there
to provide for you.' So he arose and went to
Zarephath, and when he came to the gate of the city,
behold, a widow was there gathering sticks; and he
called to her and said, 'Please get me a little water in
a jar, that I may drink.'*

*As she was going to get it, he called to her and said,
'Please bring me a piece of bread in your hand.' But
she said, 'As the LORD your God lives, I have no
bread, only a handful of flour in the bowl and a little
oil in the jar; and behold, I am gathering a few sticks
that I may go in and prepare for me and my son, that
we may eat it and die.'*

*Then Elijah said to her, 'Do not fear; go, do as you
have said, but make me a little bread cake from it first
and bring it out to me, and afterward you may make
one for yourself and for your son.*

*'For thus says the LORD God of Israel, "The bowl of
flour shall not be exhausted, nor shall the jar of oil be
empty, until the day that the LORD sends rain on the
face of the earth."*

*So she went and did according to the word of Elijah,
and she and he and her household ate for many days.
The bowl of flour was not exhausted nor did the jar of
oil become empty, according to the word of the LORD
which He spoke through Elijah* (vs. 8-16).

The widow could have doubted the prophet's word. She
could have said, "No, I won't bake a cake for you." She could
have said, "I only have enough to feed me and my son and
then we're going to die." But she didn't.

That handful of flour and those few drops of oil were

Seeds she willingly Sowed, and her obedience resulted in a life-saving miracle. And not only did this miracle meet the needs of the woman and her son, but *her* miraculous provision also became *Elijah's* provision!

Believe! Obey! Expect!

There are three aspects of this story that have meaning for us when considering God's principle of Sowing and Reaping, and expecting a miracle Harvest from Him.

1. The widow *believed* the word from the prophet.
2. She *obeyed* his instruction.
3. She *expected* God to honor His word spoken through His servant's mouth.

Belief, obedience, and expectation are three important factors for receiving the miracle you need from God.

Many times, Barbara and I have *believed* God for personal miracles. As we do, we *obey* whatever He tells us to do, and we *expect* God to perform a miracle.

I remember when we lived in San Diego with Ben when he was an infant. One day he was burning up with a fever, so we took his temperature, and it was between 104–105 degrees.

We called our pediatrician, who told us to bring Ben to the emergency room right away. (He didn't say to bring him to his *office*, but to go immediately to the emergency room at the hospital. We knew it was serious!)

Barbara and I were rushing out the door when I sensed the Holy Spirit's leading. I stopped and said to her, "Before we go, let's sit down and pray and anoint him with oil, and see what God will do." We sat down together on the couch with Ben in our arms. As we anointed him with oil, we laid hands on him and prayed the Prayer of Faith together.

While we were praying, our little baby boy literally, went

from burning up with fever to being completely cool, with no fever and a perfectly normal temperature. There was no need for us to take him to the hospital emergency room.

For two young parents with their first child, this was an amazing, miraculous intervention. Here is the simple "formula" we used:

* We *believed* in God's healing power.
* We *obeyed* the Holy Spirit and the instructions in James 5:14 to lay hands on the sick and anoint them with oil.
* We *expected* a miracle...and God did just that!

Here Comes Jesus!

In each of the following Bible stories, the person *believed* the Lord, *obeyed* what they were told to do, and *expected* a miracle. And in each case, their faith was rewarded as Jesus miraculously intervened in their lives.

* Jairus, a ruler from the synagogue, had a little girl who was dying. He came and fell at Jesus' feet, begging Him to come heal his daughter. Even when reports came of her death, Jesus said to the distraught father, "Do not be afraid: only believe." Jairus' expectation was fulfilled when the Lord raised his daughter from the dead (Mark 5:21-24; 35-42).
* A Gentile woman, who would have been considered unclean by religious Jews, had a daughter who was demonically possessed. She, too, came and fell at Jesus' feet and *"kept asking"* for Him to cast out the demon. He rewarded her faith and persistence by setting her daughter free (Mark 7:25-30).
* Short Zaccheus climbed up in a tree so he wouldn't miss seeing Jesus pass by (Luke 19:1-10). The Lord spotted the eager man and said, *"Zaccheus, hurry and come down, for*

today I must stay at your house." Zaccheus quickly came down and *"received Him gladly."*

When Jesus walked through a town, He healed *"**every** kind of disease and **every** kind of sickness among the people"* (Matthew 4:23). Nothing was too difficult for Him! *"Many followed Him, and He healed them ALL"* (Matthew 12:15).

Don't Let Jesus Pass You By

Some miracles are instantaneous. Others happen over time. Even Jesus once healed a blind man who wasn't completely healed with the "first touch":

"Taking the blind man by the hand, He brought him
out of the village; and after spitting on his eyes and
laying His hands on him, He asked him, 'Do you see
anything?' And he looked up and said, 'I see men, for I
see them like trees, walking around.' Then again He
laid His hands on his eyes; and he looked intently and
was restored, and began to see everything clearly"
(Mark 8:23-25).

But although Jesus was *willing* to do miracles for anyone, most hadn't prepared their hearts for His touch. Not everyone approached Him like Jairus, the woman with the demon-possessed daughter, or Zaccheus. And as a result, many didn't receive the miracle they needed. Jesus simply passed on by them.

How sobering to think that Jesus could pass us by! This isn't because He doesn't love us or isn't willing and able to intervene in our lives. Jesus only would pass us by because we haven't prepared our heart to receive His miracles.

On one occasion, Jesus' disciples were facing the storms of life, and they were in danger of having Jesus pass by: *"He came to them, walking on the sea; and He intended to **pass by them**"*

(Mark 6:48). The disciples cried out in fear, thinking they were seeing a ghost!

But this story has such a great ending. When the disciples finally recognized Jesus, He *"got into the boat with them, and the wind stopped; and they were utterly astonished"* (Mark 6:51).

This is exactly what Jesus wants to do in *your* life today. He wants to get in the "boat" with you—right there in the midst of your storms and difficult circumstances. And then He wants to speak a powerful word to your troubling situations, stilling the winds of adversity that the enemy has brought your way.

The devil will do everything he can to stop, thwart, or hinder God's plan for you. He will do everything he can to kill, steal, and destroy you physically, emotionally, and financially. That's his agenda. However, Jesus has come to give you an abundant life!

*"The thief comes only to steal and kill and destroy; **I came that they may have life, and have it abundantly"*** (John 10:10).

I remember when I was a student at Oral Roberts University there was a sign in the cafeteria with his motto on it that "spoke" to my spirit every time I saw it:

EXPECT A MIRACLE!

My friend, I'm urging you today to *expect* the miracle you are seeking, so that God can use you as a strong witness for His miracle-working power.

CHAPTER SEVEN
EXERCISE YOUR FAITH

WHEN WE STUDY THE BIBLICAL ACCOUNTS of miracles, we begin to see the numerous patterns and characteristics that brought them about:

Persistence, determination, brokenness, repentance, humility, seeking the Lord, prayer, refusing to be "politically correct," acknowledging God's authority, reminding Him of His past faithfulness, gratitude for answered prayer, standing on the Word of God...the list is long.

But of all these, I believe that FAITH is the most important ingredient to receiving your miracle from God.

God can do anything, in any way, at any time He chooses. He is *GOD*. I'm sure that when Joshua took the children of Israel across the Jordan River, some of them were complaining, "Moses wouldn't do it this way!" But Moses wasn't the miracle worker.

And *we're* not the miracle workers either. God is. But as I shared with you earlier, we *do* have delegated authority.

The Lord wants you to understand that your faith in Him overcomes pain and suffering. He knows what it's like to live with all the hurts, vulnerabilities, and frailties of being human.

How does He know? Because He became mortal. He wrapped Himself in human flesh with a body that was susceptible to every human weakness. By doing this, He said to us, "Because I love you, I will become like you—vulnerable, weak, and mortal."

Who, being in the form of God, thought it not robbery to be equal with God: but made himself of no reputation, and took upon him the form of a servant, and was made in the likeness of men: and being found in fashion as a man, he humbled himself, and became obedient unto death, even the death of the cross.

Wherefore God also hath highly exalted him, and given him a name which is above every name:

that at the name of Jesus every knee should bow, of things in heaven, and things in earth, and things under the earth; and that every tongue should confess that Jesus Christ is Lord, to the glory of God the Father (Philippians 2:6-11 KJV).

Jesus was obedient to His Father *"unto death."* Because of this, God honored and exalted His Son. In turn, Jesus has honored us by delegating to us His authority.

He tells us, *"I will give you the keys of the kingdom of heaven; and whatever you bind on earth shall have been bound in heaven, and whatever you loose on earth shall have been loosed in heaven"* (Matthew 16:19).

My friend, it's time for us to exercise our faith and authority!

Believe God and His Word

Believing in God and His Word is the most basic and vital command He has given to us.

The Bible teaches us that He is a God of infinite love, excellence, goodness, and holiness. When He promises, declares, or commands something in His Word, it *always* is based on His love for us. He simply asks us to believe and obey Him.

Our faith can't be based on reason, feelings, or experience.

It must be based on our Heavenly Father and His everlasting Word. It's our unbelief in His love and His inerrant Word that results in our disobedience, rebellion, and selfishness.

Of utmost priority is believing God's promise of salvation through Jesus Christ *alone*. But to receive all of God's blessings, we also must then believe in His promises regarding our healing, relationships, prosperity, or the many other good things He wants to give us.

In the New Testament alone, there are 545 references to faith, belief, and trust. In the Old Testament there is an even greater number. When God devotes a lot of space to something in His Word, we know it has great significance to Him.

So What *IS* Faith?

Whatever you're facing, know today that you can overcome your circumstances through faith in God. But what is faith? *"Now faith is the substance of things hoped for, the evidence of things not seen"* (Hebrews 11:1).

The Greek word for faith is *pistis,* which means "conviction, confidence, trust, belief, reliance, trustworthiness." Faith is…

1. The evidence of what is not visible here on earth.
2. God's creative power given to you when you accepted Jesus into your heart.
3. A piece of Heaven within you.
4. A gift from God.
5. The "title deed" to your spiritual inheritance.

The Bible says, *"He came to His own, and those who were His own did not receive Him. But as many as received Him, to them He gave the right to become children of God, even to those who believe in His name"* (John 1:11-12).

Faith is the power of God given only to His sons and

daughters to do mighty things for the glory and honor of the Lord Jesus Christ.

Before Jesus went to Heaven, He said, "*Truly, truly, I say to you, he who believes in Me, the works that I do, he will do also; and greater works than these he will do; because I go to the Father*" (John 14:12). The only way this is accomplished is through faith and the empowerment of the Holy Spirit in our lives.

It was the Holy Spirit Who empowered Jesus' life and miracles, and it's the same Holy Spirit Who will empower us. That's why Jesus told His disciples to wait in Jerusalem until they had received power from on high (Luke 24:49). Who was the source of that power? The Holy Spirit.

Believe Him

God holds us responsible for our obedience or disobedience to His commandment to believe Him and His Word.

In concise language, the writer of Hebrews tells us, "*Without faith, it is impossible to please Him, for he who comes to God must believe that He is and that He is a rewarder of those who diligently seek Him*" (Hebrews 11:6).

The Greek word most often used for "believe" is *pisteuo,* which means "to trust in, rely upon, cling to, commit to, and have conviction."

In the Old Testament, the Hebrew words most frequently used for "belief" are *batach* and *chacah*. They have almost the exact same meaning as *pisteuo,* but they are translated more frequently into English as "trust."

We can see, then, that the words for "faith," "belief," and "trust" are clearly related.

"*If you shall confess with your mouth the Lord Jesus, and shall believe in your heart that God has raised Him from the dead, you shall be saved. For with the heart man believes untorighteousness...*" (Romans 10:9-10 KJV).

Faith is not only a choice of the *mind,* but more importantly, it's a decision of the *heart.* However, God must supernaturally touch our spirit with His Holy Spirit and enable us to believe so that we can trust in His love, His grace, His mercy, and His sacrificial blood.

"For by grace are you saved through faith, and that not of yourselves, it is the gift of God, not of works, lest any man should boast" (Ephesians 2:8-9 KJV).

Child-Like Faith Is a Requirement

God and His Word are to be the focus of our faith. It's in Him that we must place our trust. God and God *alone* is eternally worthy as the Foundation and Center of our faith. For this reason, we must know the kind of God on which our faith is founded...

He is utterly perfect in every aspect of His being and nature. He is righteous, just, and true. He is pure love. He is so inexpressibly great that He is glorious! He is to be worshipped and loved to the utmost!

And as our sovereign Lord of Lords, He has made simple, child-like faith a requirement for us all.

As our understanding and knowledge of our loving Heavenly Father increases through time spent in His Word and by the revelation of His Holy Spirit...as our relationship with the Lord grows through worshipping Him, talking to Him, listening to Him, and receiving His love...then it becomes increasingly easy to believe deeply and unshakably in His promises, declarations, and commands in Scripture.

Yes, miracles are tremendous. They are for us today and greatly to be desired. But we must be careful that our enthusiasm and love is for our glorious Redeemer...and not for the miracles He performs in our midst.

In other words, we must seek the Healer and not the healing. He alone is to be glorified, not His creations. When He moves in your life with His miracle-working power, glorify *Him*, and not the miracle itself.

The Force of Faith

Faith can best be understood by its effects and results. Our faith can powerfully and beautifully affect our emotions, body, soul, mind, spirit, and actions.

Faith is a vital, spiritual force. To the leper who received his miracle, the Lord said, *"Arise, go thy way; thy **faith** hath made thee whole"* (Luke 17:19 KJV).

The **force of faith**, exercised as an act of our free will, is activated by God's supernatural power.

Earlier in this chapter, we looked at Hebrews 11:1 as the foundation for our definition of faith: *"Faith is the substance of things hoped for, the evidence of things not seen."*

Faith isn't a substance like steel or concrete, but as a spiritual force, it's as real as a piece of steel. It can't be seen, but neither can electricity, air, or the structure of the atom, about which we know a great deal.

Just as the spiritual force of faith calls forth the Divine power of God, the spiritual forces of fear and doubt call forth the power of Satan. When Adam followed Satan's rationalizations, he became vulnerable to his evil influence (Genesis 3:1-24).

After Adam disbelieved and disobeyed God, the very first words he spoke to God were, *"I heard the sound of You in the garden, and I was afraid..."* (Genesis 3:10). Since he had disbelieved God, and therefore disobeyed Him, he became vulnerable to fear and doubt.

If Adam had immediately repented and confessed his sin, God would have forgiven him. Instead, he did what most of us have done many times: he shifted the blame to someone else—Eve, who then shifted the blame to the serpent.

The forces of fear and doubt working against us in weak, unbelieving moments will try and influence us to do evil things. But if with determination and prayer, we call on Jesus' name and replace fear with faith and doubt with belief, we will experience God's promised miracle!

Ten Tools for Increasing Our Faith

None of us can boast of having a faith that is perfect in intensity, strength, or persistence. But God doesn't leave us alone in our weakness. He has given us tools to help increase our faith—and they work!

1. **ASK FOR MORE.** The 12 apostles were strong men, but they humbly begged, "INCREASE our faith!" (Luke 17:5) We, too, must humbly ask in Jesus' name for the Father to increase our faith. *"Whatsoever ye shall ask the Father in My name, He will give it to you"* (John 16:23 KJV). It is vital that we exercise whatever level of faith we already have when praying for our miracle, but then we must ask God for even *more* faith.

2. **READ GOD'S WORD.** Reading the Bible with the Holy Spirit's guidance is one of the best methods for building our faith: *"FAITH comes by hearing, and hearing by the Word of God"* (Romans 10:17 KJV). Reading Scriptures aloud on healing and faith will build your faith as you hear God's Word spoken, even when it's just your own voice you're hearing!

3. **FAST AND PRAY.** Combining fasting with prayer is a powerful weapon in our spiritual arsenal. If you find your faith being attacked by fear and doubt, fasting under the Lord's direction may be just what's needed to restore and build your faith.

4. **PRAY IN THE SPIRIT**. Praying in a supernatural lan-

guage given by the Holy Spirit is an excellent way to build our faith: *"But you, beloved, building yourselves up in your most holy FAITH, praying in the Holy Spirit, keep yourselves in the love of God…"* (Jude 1:20).

5. **SPEAK GOD'S WORD.** Spoken words have a lot of power: *"Death and life are in the power of the tongue, and those who love it will eat its fruit"* (Proverbs 18:21). Our words have power, both for good and for evil. While faith deep within the heart is vital, the words coming out of our mouths are given great weight by our Lord. Decide today that you no longer will speak discouraging or faith-destroying words but only those which are encouraging and faith-building.

6. **MOVE WITHIN GOD'S LOVE.** *"Faith working through love"* (Galatians 5:6) is one of the most effective methods for increasing our faith. When God's unconditional love is flowing in the Spirit, it's much easier for us to believe His Word. On the other hand, if there is bitterness in our lives as we're asking for God to do a miracle, His wonder-working power can be blocked.

7. **WORSHIP AND PRAISE HIM.** Worshipping and praising the Lord with love and adoration in our hearts inevitably increases our faith. *"I will call upon the Lord, who is worthy to be praised; so shall I be saved from my enemies"* (Psalm 18:3 KJV). Through praise and worship, the faith level of His children is raised, and God's miracle-working power is released!

8. **WITNESS MIRACLES.** Seeing God work miracles in the lives of others builds our faith. *"When He was in Jerusalem at the Passover, in the feast day, many believed in His name, when they saw the MIRACLES which He did"* (John 2:23 KJV). Witnessing God's miracles can even turn skeptical scientists into Believers!

9. **TESTIFY TO GOD'S POWER.** Sharing with others about Who God is, how much He loves us, and His power to

mend broken lives will increase your faith. Abraham was one of the greatest men of faith who ever lived. His faith was built and maintained by giving glory to God. *"He staggered not at the promise of God through unbelief; but was strong in faith, giving Glory to God"* (Romans 4:20 KJV).

10. **OVERCOME OBSTACLES TO FAITH.** Faith is a spiritual force. Just like the force of electricity, there are certain things that can block faith from flowing from God into our hearts and through our lives. Some obstacles to faith are willful unrepentance, rebellion against His Word, neglecting our relationship with Him, unforgiveness, and bitterness, just to name a few. How do we overcome these obstacles? Repent and ask God for the courage, strength, and power of the Holy Spirit to walk in victory in Jesus' name!

"Let This Mind Be in YOU"

Faith is vital if we want to please God: *"Without faith it is impossible to please Him…"* (Hebrews 11:6).

At the same time, we must be careful *how* we use our faith. As Believers, we are to surrender our human will to God's will (Luke 22:42). And to know His will, we must study and understand His Word, seeking His face in prayer with a devoted, loving heart.

If we neglect to do this in humility, we can tragically place our faith in the wrong thing or try to use our faith to claim things that may be outside of God's will for us or for our loved ones.

We must increasingly walk in the truth that we have the mind of Christ (1 Corinthians 2:16). We can *never* depend on the reasoning of our own minds. Instead, we need to diligently seek God's will, and then surrender to it, continually praying by faith that He will *"Let this mind be in you, which was also in Christ Jesus"* (Philippians 2:5 KJV).

Through faith, God can deliver us suddenly and supernaturally from our enemies, sicknesses, and circumstances, as He did with Peter out of the tightly-guarded jail (Acts 12:3-19) and Paul and Silas when they were imprisoned (Acts 16:25-34).

Satan will try to trick us into believing that we must live a sinless life in order to receive a miracle from God. But this is a lie. It's also impossible. That's why we need to walk continuously in the freedom and truth of God's grace and forgiveness: *"Christ redeemed us from the curse of the Law, having become a curse for us—for it is written, 'CURSED IS EVERYONE WHO HANGS ON A TREE'"* (Galatians 3:13).

Our righteousness is through faith ALONE in the Lord Jesus and the redeeming blood He shed for us on the Cross.

You Must Decide

I know many theologians who try to make the Bible complex, but to me, God's Word is simple and clear. In it, He gives us a choice, and we all must decide whether to live according to His Word or to live according to our own fleshly desires.

You must decide. If you are a child of God, then you must refuse to walk in defeat or live in poverty. You must claim your spiritual inheritance!

God's Word is clear about this inheritance: *"If you then, being evil, know how to give good gifts to your children, how much more will your Father who is in heaven give what is good to those who ask Him!"* (Matthew 7:11)

In fact, your Heavenly Father has already given you your inheritance. What has He given you?

Eternal life. Forgiveness of sin. Grace. Mercy. His Word and the promises it holds for you. The right to use His name. The right to exercise His authority over all the power of the enemy.

What's sad is that many of us either don't want to—or don't know how to—lay hold of the inheritance God has already given us. Does this describe you?

Maybe you are living life like someone with a brand new car in the garage who doesn't know how to drive. You haven't read the owner's manual, so you don't know how to operate the car or take advantage of all its great features.

Sure, you can turn the radio on, but do you know how to use all the functions and presets so that you can make the radio work? Sure, you may know how to drive from one place to another, but do you know how to use the navigation system that can provide clear instructions for getting from one point to another and keep you from getting lost?

The analogy is a simple one. To live our lives to the fullest...to take complete advantage of all the blessings God has for us...we need to read the "Owner's Manual"—the Bible—and we must understand the keys and principles by which He operates.

So many of us don't know how to "operate" the power of God or how to appropriate His miracle-working power. We don't exercise our God-given spiritual authority over all the power and influence of the devil. We don't know how to apply spiritual truths to the natural world and our circumstances, so we fail to activate God's promises in our lives.

Our faith is impoverished when we say that we're a Believer and a child of God, yet we can't—or won't—lay hold of all the amazing blessings He offers us to make us *"more than a conqueror through Him that loved us"* (Romans 8:37 KJV).

"Nothing Shall Be Impossible to You"

No matter who you are or what your circumstances are, God can give you the faith to overcome any problem you face:

"If you have faith as a grain of mustard seed, you shall say unto this mountain, be thou removed, and it shall be removed; and nothing shall be impossible to you" (Matthew 17:20 KJV).

Nothing...absolutely *NOTHING*...will be impossible for you! If you do not doubt, then whatever you are believing

God to do for you according to His will shall come to pass.

But, there is a condition: *"IF you have faith."*

Heaven is FULL of faith and is not contaminated with even one drop of unbelief. In the same way, we cannot contaminate our belief with unbelief. Belief requires having 100% faith.

Do you struggle with doubt and unbelief? Then persistently cry out to the Lord with the same words that a desperate father cried to Jesus when he begged Him to heal his son: *"And straightway the father of the child cried out, and said with tears, Lord, I believe; help thou mine unbelief"* (Mark 9:24 KJV).

Without faith, it's impossible to please God. So the way to please Him is by having faith. When you come to Him in faith, trusting in the name of Jesus and believing in Him, He is there for you!

Activate Your Faith

You know, I've heard a lot of different definitions of faith in my life, and there's one more definition I've come to embrace that I want to share with you:

FAITH IS ACTION IN OBEDIENCE TO THE PERCEIVED WORD OF GOD.

Your faith is activated by your obedience to what you believe to be God's will or instruction.

When you know God is telling you to do something, your choice is to obey or disobey Him. Faith isn't the issue, because you know what He's telling you to do. The issue is obedience.

But did you know there are times that even when you're wrong, you're right? How can that be? Because God *honors* our faith and obedience.

Imagine a child talking to a parent who is disappointed in the child's actions. Just when the "board of education" is about to be applied to the "seat of learning," the child says, "But I was just doing what I thought you told me to do."

You stop and dig a little deeper to find out what he's talking about, and you discover that even though your child did the exact opposite of your instructions, from *his* perspective, he was doing exactly what he thought you wanted.

How can a loving, rational parent still discipline their child for disobedience when the child thought he was being obedient? They can't, or at least they shouldn't. What the parent should do is use this as an opportunity to help the child learn how to listen more closely and then obey what he's told to do.

It's the same way in our relationship with our loving Heavenly Father. When we disobey Him, He looks at the motive of our heart. Were we rebelling against Him? Were we acting in outright stubbornness and disobedience? Or were we acting on what we thought He was telling us to do?

Faith is putting into action what you perceive is God's will to the best of your ability. God looks on your heart and rewards your right motives and your obedience…even when you're wrong. So today, activate your faith!

As Jesus said to the blind man (Mark 10:52), the woman with the issue of blood (Luke 8:48), and the leper (Luke 17:16-20) when He healed them, I speak this blessing over you:

YOUR FAITH HAS MADE YOU WHOLE!

CHAPTER EIGHT
RECEIVE YOUR MIRACLE

ARE YOU AT THE END OF YOUR ROPE TODAY?

In desperation, you may be saying, "Forget it. I've been believing God for my miracle for years, and it never comes, so what's the use?"

My answer for you is found in Luke 11:9: *"Ask, and it will be given to you; seek, and you will find; knock, and it will be opened unto you."*

This verse in the Greek is better translated like this: "Ask, and keep on asking. Seek, and keep on seeking. Knock, and keep on knocking."

Jesus is telling us to persevere and persist when asking God to move on our behalf. Why? Because… *"every one who asks, receives; and he who seeks, finds; and to him who knocks, it will be opened"* (v. 10).

Don't Give Up!

Nowhere is our need for perseverance in prayer better illustrated than in Jesus' parable of the widow and the unjust judge:

> *Now He was telling them a parable to show that at all times they ought to pray and not to lose heart, saying, 'In a certain city there was a judge who did not fear God and did not respect man. There was a widow in that city, and she kept coming to him, saying, "Give me legal protection from my opponent."*

'For a while he was unwilling; but afterward he said to himself, "Even though I do not fear God nor respect man, yet because this widow bothers me, I will give her legal protection, otherwise by continually coming she will wear me out."'

And the Lord said, 'Hear what the unrighteous judge said; now, will not God bring about justice for His elect who cry to Him day and night, and will He delay long over them? I tell you that He will bring about justice for them quickly. However, when the Son of Man comes, will He find faith on the earth?'
(Luke 18:1-8)

What can we learn from this persistent widow about persevering in faith for our miracle?

* She wouldn't take "NO" for an answer.
* She "bothered" the judge.
* She was determined.
* She cried out for what was rightfully hers.
* She had faith in the judge's ability to help her.
* She put works to her faith.

Isn't it interesting that this is the story Jesus used as His example for how we are to approach our Heavenly Father?

Principles for Receiving Your Miracle

There are no "fast-food, drive-through" quick fixes for a miracle. There are no shortcuts. Our God is a sovereign God Who doesn't need or use formulas. He freely employs His grace to give you the miracle you're seeking.

However, there *are* some basic Miracle Keys from the miraculous Biblical stories we looked at in Chapter 4.

And now in this chapter, I want to share with you 20

"Miracle Principles." These are practical ways to help you receive your miracle from God. Some of these I've already mentioned, and some of them I'm highlighting for the first time.

Keep in mind that every miracle does *not* happen in the same way. Have you ever heard the silly story about the man who received his miracle while standing at the kitchen stove at 3 a.m.? From then on, whenever he needed something miraculous, he would go to the stove early in the morning.

At the same time, I believe that these Miracle Principles are so vital that I urge you to follow them, and like the widow, *"Ask, and keep on asking. Seek, and keep on seeking. Knock, and keep on knocking,"* until your miracle comes or until the day you breathe your last breath!

20 Miracle Principles

1. INVITE CHRIST INTO YOUR HEART AND RECEIVE HIS JOY.

"The joy of the LORD is your strength" (Nehemiah 8:10).

"Delight yourself in the LORD; and He will give you the desires of your heart" (Psalm 37:4).

2. BELIEVE THAT IT'S GOD'S WILL FOR YOU TO RECEIVE YOUR MIRACLE.

"God also testifying with them, both by signs and wonders and by various miracles and by gifts of the Holy Spirit according to His own will" (Hebrews 2:4).

3. LET THERE BE NO DOUBT THAT JESUS CHRIST STILL HEALS TODAY!

"God was performing extraordinary miracles by the

hands of Paul, so that handkerchiefs or aprons were even carried from his body to the sick, and the diseases left them and the evil spirits went out" (Acts 19:11-12).

"...many believed in His name, observing His signs which He was doing" (John 2:23).

4. RECOGNIZE THE GREATNESS OF THE MIRACLE WORKER AND KEEP HIS COMMANDMENTS.

*"...If you will give earnest heed to the voice of the LORD your God, and do what is right in His sight, and give ear to His commandments, and keep all His statutes, I will put none of the diseases on you which I have put on the Egyptians; for **I, the LORD, am your healer**"* (Exodus 15:26).

5. HAVE A PURE HEART.

"Nevertheless the righteous will hold to his way, and he who has clean hands will grow stronger and stronger" (Job 17:9).

"...pray for one another so that you may be healed. The effective prayer of a righteous man can accomplish much" (James 5:16).

6. OBEY GOD'S SPECIFIC INSTRUCTIONS.

"My son, do not forget my teaching, but let your heart keep my commandments; for length of days and years of life and peace they will add to you" (Proverbs 3:1-2).

"For the report of your obedience has reached to all; therefore I am rejoicing over you..." (Romans 16:19).

7. PRAY AND FAST.

"Pray without ceasing" (1 Thessalonians 5:17).

"You do not have because you do not ask"(James 4:2).

"And all things you ask in prayer, believing, you will receive" (Matthew 21:22).

"Nothing will be impossible to you. But this kind does not go out except by prayer and fasting" (Matthew 17:20-21).

8. HAVE A BROKEN AND CONTRITE SPIRIT.

"...humble yourselves under the mighty hand of God, that He may exalt you at the proper time" (1 Peter 5:6).

9. REMIND GOD OF WHAT HE HAS PROMISED.

"With respect to the promise of God, he did not waver in unbelief but grew strong in faith, giving glory to God, and being fully assured that what God had promised, He was able also to perform" (Romans 4:20-21).

"Beloved, I pray that in all respects you may prosper and be in good health, just as your soul prospers" (3 John 2).

10. HAVE FAITH FOR YOUR MIRACLE.

"Without faith it is impossible to please Him, for he who comes to God must believe that He is and that He is a rewarder of those who seek Him" (Hebrews 11:6).

11. RECEIVE THE DELIVERANCE OF GOD'S WORD.

"He sent His word and healed them, and delivered them from their destructions" (Psalm 107:20).

12. CLAIM HIS PROMISES.

"Let the words of my mouth and the meditation of my heart be acceptable in Your sight" (Psalm 19:14).

"The thief comes only to steal and kill and destroy; I came that they may have life, and have it abundantly" (John 10:10).

"By His wounds (stripes) you were healed" (1 Peter 2:24-25).

"Greater is He who is in you than he who is in the world" (1 John 4:4).

13. CELEBRATE THE LORD'S SUPPER.

"For I received from the Lord that which I also delivered to you, that the Lord Jesus in the night in which He was betrayed took bread; and when He had given thanks, He broke it and said, 'This is My body, which is for you; do this in remembrance of Me.'

"In the same way He took the cup also after supper, saying, 'This cup is the new covenant in My blood; do this, as often as you drink it, in remembrance of Me.' For as often as you eat this bread and drink the cup, you proclaim the Lord's death until He comes" (1 Corinthians 11:23-26).

14. USE ANOINTING OIL.

"Is anyone among you sick? Then he must call for the elders of the church and they are to pray over him, anointing him with oil in the name of the Lord" (James 5:14-15).

15. EXERCISE LOVE.

"If I speak with the tongues of men and of angels,

but do not have love, I have become a noisy gong or a clanging cymbal" (1 Corinthians 13:1).

16. RECEIVE THE HOLY SPIRIT.

"There is one body and one Spirit, just as also you were called in one hope of your calling; one Lord, one faith, one baptism, one God and Father of all who is over all and through all and in all" (Ephesians 4:4-6).

17. PRAISE THE LORD *BEFORE* YOU SEE YOUR MIRACLE.

"Whatever is true, whatever is honorable, whatever is right, whatever is pure, whatever is lovely, whatever is of good repute, if there is any excellence and if anything worthy of praise, dwell on these things" (Philippians 4:8-9).

18. PERSEVERE AND PERSIST.

"Trust in the LORD with all your heart and do not lean on your own understanding. In all your ways acknowledge Him, and He will make your paths straight. Do not be wise in your own eyes; fear the LORD and turn away from evil. It will be healing to your body and refreshment to your bones" (*Proverbs 3:5-8*).

19. MAINTAIN AN ATTITUDE OF HOPE.

"And not only this, but we also exult in our tribulations, knowing that tribulation brings about perseverance; and perseverance, proven character; and proven character, hope; and hope does not disappoint, because the love of God has been poured out within our hearts through the Holy Spirit who was given to us" (Romans 5:3-5).

20. STAND FIRM.

*"Therefore, take up the full armor of God, so
that you will be able to resist in the evil day,
and having done everything, to stand firm"*
(Ephesians 6:13).

*"Jesus Christ is the same yesterday and today
and forever"* (Hebrews 13:8).

I challenge you to put these 20 Miracle Principles to work
in your life, and as you do, prepare to receive your miracles. I
know from first-hand experience that God can provide any
miracle you need.

I remember the time when Barbara and I were out of
work. We had no jobs, no income, and we had used every last
penny of our savings.

Quite frankly, we were broke. We didn't know how we
were going to pay the mortgage, make the car payment, or put
food on the table.

We had done everything we knew to do in the natural…we
had applied for jobs, sent out resumes, and called companies
to request interviews. We also had done all the things we knew
to do spiritually. We had prayed, fasted, and believed that God
would step into the circumstances of our financial lives with
a genuine miracle.

I can still remember going up with Barbara to the nursery
and literally breaking open Ben's piggy bank so we could pull
out enough nickels and quarters to go buy a cheap fast food
burger. That's how bad things were.

Even so, we continued to persevere and believe God for
the miraculous.

That same week, when everything looked so bleak, I received
a consulting job that paid me $3,500 for less than a day's work!

'Methods of Miracles'

There are many different kinds of miracles. But whether your problem is physical, emotional, financial, or involves a relationship, God can give you exactly what you need.

Of course, God can—and does—use medical science to heal people. I thank Him for doctors and nurses who are bringing healing to those who are hurting.

But it's important to realize the Lord uses any number of "methods" to work His miracles. Once Jesus even healed a blind man by creating balls of mud to put in his eye sockets (John 9:1-7)!

If you or a loved one needs a miracle today, take a look at some of the Scriptural methods God uses:

1. **Praying the prayer of faith.** James writes:

> *"Is anyone among you sick? Then he must call for the elders of the church and they are to pray over him, anointing him with oil in the name of the Lord; and the prayer offered in faith will restore the one who is sick, and the Lord will raise him up, and if he has committed sins, they will be forgiven him.*
>
> *"Therefore, confess your sins to one another, and pray for one another so that you may be healed. The effective prayer of a righteous man can accomplish much"* (James 5:14-16).

There is great power in the prayers of God's believing people!

2. **Anointing with oil and laying on of hands.** James says that church leaders should pray over the sick person, *"anointing him with oil in the name of the Lord."* Likewise, Jesus' disciples *"were anointing with oil many sick people*

and healing them" (Mark 6:13). And Jesus told His followers that *"they will lay hands on the sick, and they will recover"* (Mark 16:18). Oil is a picture of the Holy Spirit in Scripture, and the Lord instructs us to lay our hands on sick people to impart His healing touch.

3. **Repenting from sins.** The Bible makes it clear that not all sickness is the result of sin in a person's life (John 9:1-3), but it also indicates that sometimes sin is a factor. That's why James says of praying for the sick, *"...if he has committed sins, they will be forgiven him. Confess your sins to one another, and pray for one another so that you may be healed."*

And after Jesus healed a sick man, He warned him, "Behold, you have become well; *do not sin anymore, so that nothing worse happens to you"* (John 5:14).

4. **Taking spiritual authority over the sickness or demon in Jesus' name.** Jesus speaks of those *"who will perform a miracle in My name"* (Mark 9:39). And Peter used the authority of Jesus' name to heal a lame man at the temple gate: *"In the name of Jesus Christ the Nazarene— walk!"* (Acts 3:6)

5. **Receiving Communion.** The Lord's Supper is a beautiful picture of our Covenant Relationship with God, and healing is part of our inheritance with that Covenant. That's why Paul warns the Corinthians about the consequences of their worldly and divisive conduct when they took Communion: *"For this reason many are weak and sick, and a number sleep"* (1 Corinthians 11:30).

Instead of God's healing power being released during the Lord's Supper, the Corinthians were reaping His judgment.

6. **Using a "point of contact."** Sometimes people in the Bible used a material object as a focal point to release their faith in God. For example, the woman who suffered with a hemorrhage proclaimed, *"If I just touch His garments, I will get well"* (Mark 5:28). And Acts describes powerful miracles through the apostle Paul: *"God was performing extraordinary miracles by the hands of Paul, so that handkerchiefs or aprons were even carried from his body to the sick, and the diseases left them and the evil spirits went out"* (Acts 19:11-12).

Was there some kind of magical power in the objects that these people used as a part of their healing? No, but these objects helped them focus their faith on God's awesome ability to do miracles in their lives.

7. **The Baptism of the Holy Spirit.** Now, let me first say what I am *not* saying: I am *not* saying that we should receive the baptism of the Holy Spirit just so that we can do miracles. However, I *am* saying that receiving the indwelling of God's Holy Spirit in all His fullness, might, and power is a doorway to the full array of God's supernatural power.

Only a few weeks *before* Peter received the filling of the Spirit, he was so spiritually weak that he denied the Lord three times in one night before the cock crowed. But immediately *after* he was baptized in the Spirit, he preached a sermon where *3,000* Souls were saved (Acts 2:41)!

Then he and John laid hands on a lame man, who walked and leaped with joy (Acts 3:1-26). *Five thousand Souls* were saved that day as a direct result of this astounding display of supernatural power (Acts 4:4). The Holy Spirit will work in us in the same way today.

The Purpose of Miracles

The Word teaches that our Heavenly Father loves us so much that He also has given us gifts of supernatural power to build His Kingdom and to save people from their sins and miseries.

The highest purpose of miracles is to glorify God!

But next in significance is to inspire the Lost to believe in Jesus as their Lord and Savior. Many who witness genuine miracles are astounded, humbled, and awed, and they become Believers as a result.

God's unsearchable wonders convince many from the highest to the lowest of intellects that the Miracle Worker is the God described in the Bible. Sadly, those whose minds are blinded by pride or calloused by sin refuse to admit even what they see.

God's Word also is confirmed by His miracles: *"And they went forth and preached everywhere, the Lord working with them, and confirming the word with signs following"* (Mark 16:20 KJV).

Most people believe in Christ and receive Him as their Lord without actually seeing a miracle, but in many instances, lost Souls believe in Christ when there are clear and undeniable miracles connected with God's servants, who are teaching and preaching.

Christ rebuffed the mere desire of men to see the spectacular: *"An evil and adulterous generation seeketh after a sign"* (Matthew 12:38-39 KJV). Yet when no one demanded a wondrous sign, Jesus chose to perform many miracles out of His infinite love for us.

Lastly, let me close this chapter by saying that as important as miracles are, if we do not have love, we are *"a noisy gong"*:

If I speak with the tongues of men and of angels, but do not have love, I have become a noisy gong or a clanging cymbal. If I have the gift of prophecy, and know all mysteries and all knowledge; and if I have all faith, so as to remove mountains, but do not have love, I am nothing (1 Corinthians 13:1-2).

Friend, as we pursue God and the miracle blessings He wants to give us as His beloved children, let's remember that as with all of His gifts to us, *"the greatest of these is love"* (1 Corinthians 13:13).

Amen? Amen.

CHAPTER NINE

GREAT EXPECTATIONS

MY GOAL FOR THIS BOOK is to build faith and expectancy for you to receive your miracle from God. But I wouldn't be honest with you if I didn't pause to consider that there are those Believers who pass on from this life to the next without ever receiving their miracle.

Why?

Honestly, I wish I knew. This is one of the questions that will be at the top of my list when I get to Heaven.

For some people, it's just a matter of time. Some receive their miracle instantly. For others, their miracle comes eventually. And for still others, it doesn't come at all on this side of Heaven.

In response to our heartfelt cry for God to give us the miracle we're desperately seeking, sometimes God is our loving Daddy Who says, "Yes."

Sometimes as our loving Daddy, He says, "Wait."

And sometimes as our loving Daddy, He says, "No."

Many people want a miracle even when they've been living foolishly by not following God's Scriptural principles for their bodies, finances, or relationships. We have a vital responsibility to live according to the principles He has given. While your miracle *is* His will, He also wants you to make Godly choices.

And the truth is that sometimes Jesus performed miracles on people whose lives were a real mess and who weren't living a Godly life at all!

But the reality is that not everyone experiences a miracle from God in this lifetime. He doesn't always answer our prayers the way we wish He would. Sometimes there are reasons for this that we can understand, and sometimes there are no understandable reasons.

If we just could see as God sees, we'd learn never to question Him. But we *can't* see as God sees, and we *don't* know all that is happening "behind the scenes" that may be influencing the circumstances in our lives.

I don't have a good answer for those who love the Lord, serve Him with all their hearts to the best of their ability, obey His commandments, and live for Him, yet never receives their miracle.

They have clean hands and a pure heart before the Lord. They're doing all the things they know to do…anointing with oil, calling for the elders to lay hands on the sick, praying the Prayer of Faith, agreeing together in prayer, and yet their spouse or child still dies.

What is the explanation? I don't know. But I do know that just because their miracle doesn't happen, it doesn't mean that we stop exercising our faith, stop praying, stop persisting, stop believing, stop standing on the Word of God, stop anointing with oil, stop praying the prayer of faith, or doing all the things that God has said in His Word to do.

Fight the Good Fight

What happens if we don't receive the answer we expected? Are we a failure? No. Is God a failure? Absolutely not. God knows something that we don't know. He sees something we can't see.

This isn't meant to sound like a cop-out answer; it's just meant to say that we don't always understand why the miraculous doesn't happen. Someday, we will understand, but for right now, *"we see in a mirror dimly, but then face to face; now I know in part, but then I will know fully just as I also have been fully known"* (1 Corinthians 13:12).

In the meantime, fight the good fight. Press on. Persevere. Run the race. Reach for the prize. Don't stop doing the things that God's Word admonishes you to do. If you see the answer come, praise God. And if you don't see the answer come, praise God anyway.

Like Job, cry out, *"Though he slay me, yet will I trust in him"* (Job 13:15 KJV). The enemy had stolen Job's wealth, his health, his finances, and his family. He was stripped of everything, but when his wife told him to curse God and die, he refused. He knew that God was still God, no matter what.

God is still God, even when there are no signs of miraculous or supernatural activity. He is worthy and deserves our praise and our honor and everything we can possibly give Him, in spite of our unanswered prayers.

Believe that God derives *no* pleasure from seeing His children suffer (Ezekiel 18:32). Even though you may not get the miracle you need, God's heart is *always* toward you. This is an important promise to hang on to while waiting for your miracle.

Turn Your Eyes Upon Jesus

I want to comfort you in this. God is your loving, caring, Heavenly Father. Your miracle IS His will. Remember, the Lord *wants* us to prosper and be in health: *"Beloved, I pray that in all respects you may prosper and be in good health, just as your soul prospers"* (3 John 2).

But again, we don't always see as God sees and we don't always receive the answer we're praying and believing for. We can be obedient and earnestly work every key, principle, and method I've shared in this book to experience our miracle, but the timing is still mandated by God's sovereign will.

If God doesn't give you your miracle, KEEP PRAYING! KEEP BELIEVING! KEEP STANDING!

*"Therefore, take up the full armor of God, so that you will be able to resist in the evil day, and having done everything, to **stand firm**"* (Ephesians 6:13).

When you have done everything there is to do, you just stand on the Word of God. Say, "God said it. I believe it. That settles it!" Let God be true, and every man a liar (Romans 3:2).

We need to get our eyes off of our circumstances, and realize Who we're calling upon. As that wonderful old hymn says...

> *Turn your eyes upon Jesus,*
> *Look full in His wonderful face,*
> *And the things of earth will grow strangely dim,*
> *In the light of His glory and grace.*
> —Helen H. Lemmel

Don't Give Up!

If God doesn't answer your prayers the way you plead with Him to, it's not because He loves you or cares for you any less than His other precious sons and daughters. There is a reason that you may never know until you can ask Him face to face. In the meantime...don't give up!

The widow persisted in bothering and pestering the judge. She didn't give up.

Jacob is another one who refused to give up. He wrestled with an angel all night long, refusing to let go until he received his blessing (Genesis 32:24-30). There was determination, persistence, and perseverance in Jacob. He refused to give up until he received what he was desperately seeking.

We must have this same attitude toward God when we pray. "God, I'm not giving up! I refuse to take 'No' for an answer." Maybe it seems disrespectful or even sacrilegious to talk to God like this, but this is one of the ways that Jesus taught us to approach our Heavenly Father.

Why would God want to give you your miracle today? Because…

1. He can.
2. He loves you.
3. You are His child.
4. You are asking in faith, believing.
5. You are broken and contrite.
6. You are persisting and persevering.
7. God is God!

So turn your eyes upon Jesus today, and every day, as you gaze at Him and wait for His miracle to be released in your life. As you wait, rest in His love. Like the psalmist David, trust Him:

"I would have despaired unless I had believed that I would see the goodness of the LORD in the land of the living. Wait for the LORD; be strong and let your heart take courage; yes, wait for the LORD" (Psalm 27:13-14).

Wait for the Lord, my friend, and you *WILL* see His goodness in the land of the living.

CHAPTER TEN

STAND FIRM!

IN THIS FINAL CHAPTER, I want to share with you a significant truth...one about which so many Believers are sadly and dangerously unaware, but it is a truth that is so significant, so powerful, it truly can make the difference between receiving your God-appointed miracle or forfeiting it to the devil's strategies to steal, kill, and destroy God's plans for you (John10:10).

You see, we're living in the NATURAL WORLD where we use our five senses to see, touch, taste, hear, and smell...and we're living in the SPIRITUAL WORLD where a battle continually rages.

But did you know that the spiritual world is more real than the natural world? This natural world is dying, and everything in it will one day be gone forever:

"For all that is in the world—the lust of the flesh, the lust of the eyes, and the pride of life—is not of the Father but is of the world. And the world is passing away, and the lust of it; but he who does the will of God abides forever" (1 John 2:16-17).

Wars are being fought around the natural world right now, and we need to understand that there's also a fierce war being waged right now in the *spiritual* realm.

The devil is just as real as God, and he has a lot of power. Jesus, the Creator of the entire universe, calls him *"the ruler of this world"* (John 12:31; 16:11).

But as I've already shared with you, the devil only rules us if we *give* him control. If we don't grant him authority over our lives, he doesn't have any power over us.

Scripture states, *"He who is **in you** is **greater** than he who is* *in the world"* (1 John 4:4). What a powerful truth! As Believers, Jesus Christ is living *inside* you and me. This means that we have *His* wisdom, *His* strength, *His* courage, and *His* power to fight against the devil and his evil battle strategies.

But if we want to receive God's miracles, we need to start using the spiritual weapons of warfare He's given us.

It's Time to Get Serious

Matthew 11:12 says that the Kingdom of Heaven suffers violence, and the violent take it by force. Instead of having a DEFENSIVE strategy against the enemy as you fight for the miracle you need, you must have an OFFENSIVE battle plan to claim what is rightfully yours as God's child and to take back what the devil has stolen from you.

As you now know, God has delegated His authority to His Son, Who in turn has delegated His authority to us: *"All authority has been given to Me in heaven and earth…Peace to you. As the Father has sent Me, I also send you"* (Matthew 28:18; John 20:21).

Jesus is saying, "Just like My Dad sent Me, now I'm sending *you* with My power and authority." He's sending you out as the enemy's ADVERSARY.

An adversary is someone who actively, aggressively, and offensively opposes an enemy. It's time for the Body of Christ—for you and me—to get serious and actively, aggressively, and offensively oppose the devil.

Jesus also said that what we bind on this earth will be bound in Heaven, and what we loose on this earth will be loosed in Heaven (Matthew 16:19). However, this won't happen unless we exercise the authority we've been given.

The words we speak are power-filled. For this reason, I encourage you to memorize this Scripture verse, and then declare it OUT LOUD as you wage spiritual warfare against the enemy for your miracle:

"'No weapon formed against you shall prosper, and every tongue which rises against you in judgment you shall condemn. This is the heritage of the servants of the LORD, and their righteousness is from Me' says the LORD" (Isaiah 54:17).

You Have a Choice

Do **not** allow yourself to be overcome by spirits of apathy, defeat, or fear as you pursue God for the miracle you so desperately need. God hasn't given you a spirit of fear, but He *has* given you a spirit of love, power, and a sound mind (2 Timothy 1:7).

You have a choice today: You can sit back and do nothing and let the enemy steal, kill, and destroy your miracle. Or, you can take up your weapons of spiritual warfare and begin waging war against the enemy in the name of the Lord Jesus Christ.

My friend, God wants you to put on His full armor, and then STAND!

*"Finally, be strong in the Lord and in the strength of His might. Put on the full armor of God, so that you will be able to **STAND FIRM** against the schemes of the devil.*

"For our struggle is not against flesh and blood, but against the rulers, against the powers, against the world forces of this darkness, against the spiritual forces of wickedness in the heavenly places.

*"Therefore, take up the full armor of God, so that you will be able to resist in the evil day, and having done everything, to **STAND FIRM**.*

*"**STAND FIRM** therefore, having girded your loins*

with truth, and having put on the breastplate of righteousness, and having shod your feet with the preparation of the Gospel of peace; in addition to all, taking up the shield of faith with which you will be able to extinguish all the flaming missiles of the evil one. And take the helmet of salvation, and the sword of the Spirit, which is the word of God.

"With all prayer and petition pray at all times in the Spirit, and with this in view, be on the alert with all perseverance and petition for all the saints (Ephesians 6:10-18).

The Word of God clearly teaches that prayer is a vital piece of spiritual warfare. To defeat the enemy, we must skillfully and effectively use the sword of the Spirit, *"which is the word of God"* when we pray.

Prayer is a creative force, and it changes things. Effective prayers based soundly on God's Word and empowered by the Holy Spirit are miracle-working prayers!

Prayer Is as Vital as Breath!

No living thing can survive without air, and no Believer can exist without prayer. It's as vital as breath itself. All answered prayer involves the supernatural.

Prayer is our very lifeline to the God of love, mercy, grace, and MIRACLES.

We are commanded to pray:

"Ask, and it shall be given to you; seek, and you shall find; knock, and it shall be opened unto you; for everyone who asks, receives; and he who seeks, finds; and he who knocks, it shall be opened" (Matthew 7:7-8).

"Pray without ceasing" (1 Thessalonians 5:17).

"Watch and pray, that you enter not into temptation; the spirit indeed is willing, but the flesh is weak" (Matthew 26:41).

"I exhort, therefore, that first of all, supplications, prayers, intercessions, and giving of thanks be made for all men" (1 Timothy 2:1).

We Must Pray With Faith:

"Without faith, it is impossible to please Him; for he who cometh to God, must believe that He is, and that He is a rewarder of those who diligently seek Him" (Hebrews 11:6).

"Whatsoever things you desire, when you pray, BELIEVE that you shall receive them, and you shall have them" (Mark 11:24).

As You Pray, God's Joy and Peace Will Be Yours:

"Ask and you shall receive, that your joy may be full" (John 16:24).

"Delight yourself also in the Lord, and He shall give you the desires of your heart" (Psalm 37:4).

"Be anxious for nothing, but in everything by prayer and supplication with thanksgiving, let your requests be known unto God. And the peace of God that passes all understanding shall keep your hearts and minds through Christ Jesus" (Philippians 4:6).

Touching God's Heart

God desires to pour His love out on you through the miracle of answered prayer, so as you pray, be specific about what you are asking Him to do for you.

Not all prayer needs to be dramatic and highly emotional, but prayers that don't come from our heart and aren't prayed with faith have little chance of being answered by God.

There are many Scriptures, especially in the Psalms of David, which reveal how our prayers never need to be routine, formal, or lifeless. Take the time to read through these songs, which really were heartfelt cries, born out of desperate circumstances and a passion to experience the Presence and Power of the Living God.

We must pray passionate prayers from a passionate heart, knowing that we have the ability to touch the heart of our compassionate, personal God.

To receive your miracle, keep your heart tender and responsive before your loving Heavenly Father, a heart through which your miracle will come easily.

Through prayer, you can live an overcoming and victorious life filled with tenderness and intimacy with the Lord. Prayer is the beautiful means through which you can directly experience His infinite glory, mercy, love, holiness, and goodness. Let's pray together right now:

Dear Heavenly Father,

Thank You for Your love and Your mercy.
Thank You that Your heart's desire is to bless
Your children with Your Power, Your Presence, Your
Peace, and Your Provision.

Father, I'm asking You in Jesus' name to step
into the circumstances of Your precious child's
situation. Demonstrate Yourself strong on their behalf.
You know their hurt. You know their pain. You know
precisely the absolute miracle that
needs to take place in their life for them to live
in complete victory. I'm asking You to do it now,
in the mighty Name of Jesus.

*Give them a personal visitation of Your Holy Spirit.
Touch them at the exact point of their need. By faith,
we believe it is done!*

In Jesus' Mighty Name. Amen.

Get Ready for Miracles!

Friend, I've never felt it so strongly: Jesus is passing this way. He wants to give you the miracles you need in your...

* Marriage
* Children
* Finances
* Health
* Job
* Relationships

It's time to prepare your heart. It's time to stir your faith with expectancy. It's time to commit to a faith-filled, obedient, love relationship with Him.

Reach out and touch the hem of Jesus' garment today. Cry out to Him in faith like blind Bartimaeus. Don't let anything hold you back from receiving everything God wants to do in your life.

Through the work the Lord has done in me and because of what He has taught me throughout the years, God has given me a measure of understanding and wisdom, which I wanted to share with you. In this book, I've done my best to impart to you the same principles I practice in my own life.

As you do the things I'm encouraging you to do, you can rest in the Lord, confident in His love, knowing that He is the only One Who can meet all your needs, and trusting that He *wants* to pour His miracle blessings into your life.

Let's join our faith. Let's join our prayers. Let's believe

together for God to release His supernatural, miracle-working power in your life:

"If two of you agree on earth about anything that they may ask, it shall be done for them by My Father who is in heaven. For where two or three have gathered together in My name, there I am there in their midst" (Matthew 18:19-20).

Together, we will stay in prayer and constant communication with our Heavenly Father, the Miracle Worker, Who loves and cares for us more than we can possibly comprehend.

Please know that we're in complete agreement with you for your complete miracle to come to pass. Barbara and I would love to hear from you, so that we can continue to pray this Prayer of Agreement with you from Matthew 18:19 and believe God for your miracle.

And so that you can be an encouragement to others, we also would love for you to share your testimony of God's miracle answers to your prayers!

You can contact us through the mail or our website at:

> David and Barbara Cerullo
> Inspiration Ministries
> P.O. Box 7750
> Charlotte, NC 28241 USA
> www.inspiration.org

Or call our Inspiration Prayer Center at 803-578-1800 to speak with one of our Prayer Ministers.

Know that Barbara and I love you, and we're praying for you. Great things are ahead as we serve the Lord together for the glory of His Kingdom.

God Bless You!